THIS IS THE CHRISTIAN FAITH

Written by *RICHARD J. SCHULTZ*

Illustrated by *BETTY WIND*

CONCORDIA CATECHISM SERIES
Walter M. Wangerin, EDITOR

CONCORDIA CATECHISM SERIES

PRIMARY LEVEL

God Loves You
God Makes Me His Child in Baptism
God Invites Me to Pray
God Gives Me His Law
God Made You Somebody Special
God Comes to Me in My Worship

ADVANCED LEVEL

When God Chose Man
This Is the Christian Faith
And Live Under Him

Authorized by The Lutheran Church — Missouri Synod for development by the Board of Parish Education, Arthur L. Miller, executive secretary, guided by the catechism committee: Harry G. Coiner, Frederick Nohl, Arnold C. Mueller, Waldemar W. Affeldt, Lewis C. Niemoeller.

Concordia Publishing House, St. Louis, Missouri
Concordia Publishing House Ltd., London, E. C. 1
© 1967 by Concordia Publishing House
Manufactured in the United States of America

The Christian faith is not something old and dead in a museum. It is as new and alive as the Christians who believe it. It is as alive as the risen Lord Jesus Christ. St. Paul says faith is like a shield.

> Above all taking the shield of faith, with which you can quench all the flaming darts of the Evil One. Ephesians 6:16

God's powerful and cruel enemies wage bitter war against all believers. They attack us time after time. God gives us equipment to conquer the Evil One. One part of this equipment is the shield of faith.

This reminds us of the title of this catechism you are about to study. This is the Christian faith as Dr. Martin Luther outlined its teachings in his Small Catechism. This is Book 2 of three catechisms.

Book 1 relates the history of God's plan of salvation. The lessons take their order from the account of the acts of God in the Holy Scriptures. I hope you studied this catechism last year. Book 3 teaches about the worship life of the child of God, and the lessons follow the church year.

A companion book to this catechism is your Pupil Guide. Your faithful use of it will make the message of the catechism more meaningful to you. Your teacher's copy of the catechism includes many ideas to help you in the classes.

The lessons follow the historic outline of Christian doctrine: the Ten Commandments, the Apostles' Creed, the Lord's Prayer, and the Sacraments of Holy Baptism and Holy Communion.

I pray that your study of God's acts for you as described in this catechism will give the Holy Spirit the opportunity to shine up your shield of faith. May the victory of our Lord Jesus Christ help you win your victories of faith.

Walter M. Wangerin, EDITOR

CONTENTS

Editor's Preface   3

Small Catechism   9

The Practice of Absolution and Confession   25

SECTION I: *Introduction*

  1. My Place in God's Plan   30

  2. My God Cares About Me   34

  3. My God Speaks to Me   39

SECTION II: *The Ten Commandments*

  4. My God Has Revealed His Law   44

  5. He Is the Lord, My God   48

  6. I Believe in the Lord, My God   52

  7. The First Commandment   56

  8. The Second Commandment   60

  9. The Third Commandment   64

10. The Fourth Commandment   68

11. The Fifth Commandment   72

12. The Sixth Commandment   76

13. The Seventh Commandment   80

14. The Eighth Commandment   84

15. The Ninth and Tenth Commandments   88

16. The Conclusion of the Commandments   92

17. Gladly Do What He Commands   96

18. Law and Gospel   100

19. Proclaiming Law and Gospel   104

SECTION III: *The Apostles' Creed*

20. The Creeds of the Church   110

21. God, the Maker of All   114

22. God, the Provider and Protector   118

23. Thank God for His Goodness   122

24. Our Lord Jesus Christ   126

25. Jesus Is God and Man   130

26. Jesus, Our Redeemer   134

27. Prophet, Priest, and King   138

28. That I May Be His Own   142

29. The Holy Spirit   146

30. The Holy Spirit at Work in Me 150
31. The Holy Christian Church 151
32. Where Is the Church? 158
33. The Broken Church 162
34. The Church in Action 166
35. The Resurrection of the Body 170
36. Eternal Life 174

SECTION IV: *The Lord's Prayer*

37. Christian Prayer 180
38. Praying to Our Father 184
39. Hallow God's Name 188
40. May God's Kingdom Come 192
41. God's Will Be Done 196
42. Our Father and Our Daily Bread 200
43. Forgiven and Forgiving 204
44. The Christian's Help in Battle 208
45. Set Free from Evil's Power 212
46. It Shall Be So 216

SECTION V: *Word and Sacraments*

47. God's Means of Grace 222
48. What Is Baptism? 226
49. Baptism's Blessings and Power 230
50. Baptism in Our Daily Lives 234
51. What Is the Sacrament of the Altar? 238
52. The Blessings and Power of the Lord's Supper 242
53. Getting Ready for the Sacrament 246
54. Claiming God's Promises 250
55. Ambassadors for Christ 254
56. The Special Ministry 258
57. Mutual Care and Discipline 262
58. Confession and Absolution 266

SECTION VI: *Living for Jesus*

59. The Fruit of the Spirit in the Christian Life 272
60. Growing as a Christian 276
61. The Christian Life of Worship 280
62. Living Witnesses of the Living Lord 284

The Small Catechism

PART ONE
The Ten Commandments

I am the Lord your God.

THE FIRST COMMANDMENT

You shall have no other gods.

What does this mean for us?

We are to fear, love, and trust God above anything else.

THE SECOND COMMANDMENT

You shall not take the name of the Lord your God in vain.

What does this mean for us?

We are to fear and love God
so that we do not use His name superstitiously, or use it
to curse, swear, lie, or deceive,
but call on Him in prayer, praise, and thanksgiving.

THE THIRD COMMANDMENT

Remember the Sabbath Day, to keep it holy.

What does this mean for us?

We are to fear and love God
so that we do not neglect His Word and the preaching of it,
but regard it as holy
and gladly hear and learn it.

THE FOURTH COMMANDMENT

Honor your father and your mother.

What does this mean for us?

We are to fear and love God
so that we do not despise or anger our parents and others in authority,
but respect, obey, love, and serve them.

THE FIFTH COMMANDMENT

You shall not kill.

What does this mean for us?

We are to fear and love God
so that we do not hurt our neighbor in any way,
but help him in all his physical needs.

THE SIXTH COMMANDMENT

You shall not commit adultery.

What does this mean for us?

We are to fear and love God
so that in matters of sex our words and conduct are pure and
    honorable,
and husband and wife love and respect each other.

THE SEVENTH COMMANDMENT

You shall not steal.

What does this mean for us?

We are to fear and love God
so that we do not take our neighbor's money or property,
or get them in any dishonest way,
but help him to improve and protect
his property and means of making a living.

THE EIGHTH COMMANDMENT

You shall not bear false witness against your neighbor.

What does this mean for us?

We are to fear and love God
so that we do not betray, slander, or lie about our neighbor,
but defend him, speak well of him, and explain his actions in the
    kindest way.

THE NINTH COMMANDMENT

You shall not covet your neighbor's house.

What does this mean for us?

We are to fear and love God
so that we do not desire to get our neighbor's possessions by
scheming,
or by pretending to have a right to them,
but always help him keep what is his.

THE TENTH COMMANDMENT

You shall not covet your neighbor's wife or his man-servant or his maidservant or his cattle or anything that is your neighbor's.

What does this mean for us?

We are to fear and love God
so that we do not tempt or coax away from our neighbor his wife
or his workers,
but encourage them to remain loyal.

What does God say of all these commandments?

He says:
"I, the Lord your God, am a jealous God,
visiting the iniquity of the fathers upon the children to the third
and fourth generation of those who hate Me,
but showing steadfast love to thousands of those who love Me and
keep My commandments."

What does this mean for us?

God warns that He will punish all who break these commandments;
therefore we are to fear His wrath and not disobey Him.
But He promises grace and every blessing to all who keep these
commandments;
therefore we are to love and trust Him, and gladly do what He
commands.

PART TWO
The Apostles' Creed

THE FIRST ARTICLE

**I believe in God the Father Almighty,
Maker of heaven and earth.**

What does this mean?

I believe that God has created me and all that exists.
He has given me and still preserves
my body and soul with all their powers.
He provides me with food and clothing, home and family, daily work,
    and all I need from day to day.
God also protects me in time of danger and guards me from every
    evil.
All this He does out of fatherly and divine goodness and mercy,
    though I do not deserve it.
Therefore I surely ought to thank and praise, serve and obey Him.
This is most certainly true.

THE SECOND ARTICLE

**And in Jesus Christ,
His only Son, our Lord;
who was conceived by the Holy Ghost,
born of the Virgin Mary;
suffered under Pontius Pilate,
was crucified, dead, and buried;
He descended into hell;
the third day He rose again from the dead;
He ascended into heaven,
and sitteth on the right hand of God the Father Almighty;
from thence He shall come to judge the quick and the
    dead.**

What does this mean?

I believe that Jesus Christ—
true God, Son of the Father from eternity,
and true man, born of the Virgin Mary—
is my Lord.
At great cost He has saved and redeemed me, a lost and condemned
person.
He has freed me from sin, death, and the power of the devil—
not with silver or gold,
but with His holy and precious blood
and His innocent suffering and death.
All this He has done that I may be His own,
live under Him in His kingdom,
and serve Him in everlasting righteousness, innocence, and blessedness,
just as He is risen from the dead and lives and rules eternally.
This is most certainly true.

THE THIRD ARTICLE

I believe in the Holy Ghost;
the holy Christian church, the communion of saints;
the forgiveness of sins;
the resurrection of the body;
and the life everlasting. Amen.

What does this mean?

I believe that I cannot by my own understanding or effort
believe in Jesus Christ, my Lord, or come to Him.
But the Holy Spirit has called me through the Gospel,
enlightened me with His gifts,
and sanctified and kept me in true faith.
In the same way He calls, gathers, enlightens, and sanctifies
the whole Christian church on earth,
and keeps it united with Jesus Christ in the one true faith.
In this Christian church day after day
He fully forgives my sins
and the sins of all believers.

On the last day He will raise me and all the dead
and give me and all believers in Christ eternal life.
This is most certainly true.

PART THREE
The Lord's Prayer

THE INTRODUCTION

Our Father who art in heaven.

What does this mean?

Here God encourages us to believe
that He is truly our Father
and we are His children.
We therefore are to pray to Him with complete confidence
just as children speak to their loving father.

THE FIRST PETITION

Hallowed be Thy name.

What does this mean?

God's name certainly is holy in itself,
but we ask in this prayer
that we may keep it holy.

When does this happen?

God's name is hallowed
whenever His Word is taught in its truth and purity
and we as children of God live in harmony with it.
Help us to do this, heavenly Father!

But anyone who teaches or lives contrary to the Word of God
dishonors God's name among us.
Keep us from doing this, heavenly Father!

THE SECOND PETITION

Thy kingdom come.

What does this mean?

God's kingdom comes indeed
without our praying for it,
but we ask in this prayer
that it may come also to us.

When does this happen?

God's kingdom comes
when our heavenly Father gives us His Holy Spirit,
so that by His grace we believe His holy Word
and live a godly life on earth now and in heaven forever.

THE THIRD PETITION

Thy will be done on earth as it is in heaven.

What does this mean?

The good and gracious will of God is surely done without our prayer,
but we ask in this prayer
that it may be done also among us.

When does this happen?

God's will is done when He hinders and defeats every evil scheme
    and purpose
of the devil, the world, and our sinful self,
which would prevent us from keeping His name holy
and would oppose the coming of His kingdom.
And His will is done
when He strengthens our faith
and keeps us firm in His Word as long as we live.
This is His gracious and good will.

THE FOURTH PETITION

Give us this day our daily bread.

What does this mean?

God gives daily bread, even without our prayer, to all people, though
   sinful,
but we ask in this prayer
that He will help us to realize this
and to receive our daily bread with thanks.

What is meant by "daily bread"?

Daily bread includes everything needed for this life,
such as food and clothing, home and property,
work and income, a devoted family,
an orderly community, good government,
favorable weather, peace and health,
a good name, and true friends and neighbors.

THE FIFTH PETITION

And forgive us our trespasses,
As we forgive those who trespass against us.

What does this mean?

We ask in this prayer
that our Father in heaven would not hold our sins against us
and because of them refuse to hear our prayer.
And we pray that He would give us everything by grace,
for we sin every day
and deserve nothing but punishment.
So we on our part will heartily forgive
and gladly do good to those who sin against us.

THE SIXTH PETITION

And lead us not into temptation.

16

What does this mean?

God tempts no one to sin,
but we ask in this prayer that God would watch over us and keep us
so that the devil, the world, and our sinful self may not deceive us
and draw us into false belief, despair, and other great and shameful
    sins.
And we pray that even though we are so tempted
we may still win the final victory.

THE SEVENTH PETITION

But deliver us from evil.

What does this mean?

We ask in this inclusive prayer
that our heavenly Father would save us from every evil to body and
    soul,
and at our last hour would mercifully take us
from the troubles of this world to Himself in heaven.

THE DOXOLOGY

For Thine is the kingdom
and the power and the glory
forever and ever.
Amen.

What does "Amen" mean?

Amen means *Yes, it shall be so.*
We say *Amen* because we are certain
that such petitions are pleasing to our Father in heaven and are
    heard by Him.
For He Himself has commanded us to pray in this way
and has promised to hear us.

PART FOUR
The Sacrament of Holy Baptism

1

What is Baptism?

Baptism is not water only,
but it is water used together with God's Word and by His command.

What is this word?

In Matthew 28 our Lord Jesus Christ says:
"Go therefore and make disciples of all nations,
baptizing them in the name of the Father and of the Son and of the
    Holy Spirit."

2

What benefits does God give in Baptism?

In Baptism God forgives sin,
delivers from death and the devil,
and gives everlasting salvation to all who believe what He has promised.

What is God's promise?

In Mark 16 our Lord Jesus Christ says:
"He who believes and is baptized will be saved;
but he who does not believe will be condemned."

3

How can water do such great things?

It is not water that does these things,
but God's Word with the water and our trust in this Word.
Water by itself is only water,
but with the Word of God it is a life-giving water
which by grace gives the new birth through the Holy Spirit.
St. Paul writes in Titus 3:
"He saved us . . . in virtue of His own mercy,
by the washing of regeneration and renewal in the Holy Spirit,

which He poured out upon us richly
through Jesus Christ our Savior,
so that we might be justified by His grace
and become heirs in hope of eternal life.
The saying is sure."

4

What does Baptism mean for daily living?

It means that our sinful self, with all its evil deeds and desires,
should be drowned through daily repentance;
and that day after day a new self should arise
to live with God in righteousness and purity forever.
St. Paul writes in Romans 6:
"We were buried therefore with Him by Baptism into death,
so that as Christ was raised from the dead by the glory of the Father,
we too might walk in newness of life."

✠　　✠　　✠

PART FIVE
The Sacrament of Holy Communion

1

What is Holy Communion?

Holy Communion is the body and blood of
our Lord Jesus Christ given with bread
and wine, instituted by Christ Himself
for us to eat and drink.

Where do the Scriptures say this?

Matthew, Mark, Luke, and Paul say:
Our Lord Jesus Christ, in the night in which He was betrayed,
took bread; and when He had given thanks,
He broke it and gave it to His disciples,
saying, "Take, eat; this is My body, which is given for you;
this do in remembrance of Me."

After the same manner also He took the cup after supper,
and when He had given thanks,
He gave it to them, saying,
"Drink of it, all of you;
this cup is the new testament in My blood,
which is shed for you and for many for the remission of sins;
this do, as often as you drink it, in remembrance of Me."

2

What benefits do we receive from this sacrament?

The benefits of this sacrament are pointed out by the words,
given and shed for you for the remission of sins.
These words assure us that in the sacrament
we receive forgiveness of sins, life, and salvation.
For where there is forgiveness of sins,
there is also life and salvation.

3

How can eating and drinking do all this?

It is not eating and drinking that does this,
but the words, *given and shed for you for the remission of sins.*
These words, along with eating and drinking, are the main thing in
    the sacrament.
And whoever believes these words
has exactly what they say, forgiveness of sins.

4

When is a person rightly prepared to receive this sacrament?

Fasting and other outward preparations serve a good purpose.
However, that person is well prepared and worthy who believes these
    words,
given and shed for you for the remission of sins.
But anyone who does not believe these words, or doubts them,
is neither prepared nor worthy,
for the words *for you* require simply a believing heart.

✠   ✠   ✠

20

PART SIX
The Office of the Keys

What is the "Office of the Keys"?

It is that authority which Christ gave to His church
to forgive the sins of those who repent
and to declare to those who do not repent
that their sins are not forgiven.

What are the words of Christ?

Our Lord Jesus Christ said to His disciples:
"Receive the Holy Spirit. If you forgive the sins of
any, they are forgiven; if you retain the sins of any,
they are retained." (John 20:23)

"Truly, I say to you, Whatever you bind on earth shall
be bound in heaven, and whatever you loose on earth
shall be loosed in heaven." (Matthew 18:18)

✠　　✠　　✠

Confession

What is private confession?

Private confession has two parts. First, we make a personal confession of sins to the pastor, and then we receive absolution,
which means forgiveness as from God Himself. This absolution
we should not doubt, but firmly believe that thereby our sins are
forgiven before God in heaven.

What sins should we confess?

Before God we should confess that we are guilty of all sins, even
those which are not known to us, as we do in the Lord's Prayer.
But in private confession, as before the pastor, we should confess only those sins which trouble us in heart and mind.

What are such sins?

We can examine our everyday life according to the Ten Commandments—for example, how we act toward father or mother, son or daughter, husband or wife, or toward the people with whom we work, and so on. We may ask ourselves whether we have been disobedient or unfaithful, bad-tempered or dishonest, or whether we have hurt anyone by word or deed.

How might we confess our sins privately?

We may say that we wish to confess our sins and to receive absolution in God's name. We may begin by saying, "I, a poor sinner, confess before God that I am guilty of many sins." Then we should name the sins that trouble us. We may close the confession with the words, "I repent of all these sins and pray for mercy. I promise to do better with God's help."

What if we are not troubled by any special sins?

We should not torture ourselves with imaginary sins. If we cannot think of any sins to confess (which would hardly ever happen), we need not name any in particular, but may receive absolution because we have already made a general confession to God.

How may we be assured of forgiveness?

The pastor may pronounce the absolution by saying, "By the authority of our Lord Jesus Christ I forgive you your sins in the name of the Father and of the Son and of the Holy Spirit. Amen."

Those who are heavily burdened in conscience the pastor may comfort and encourage with further assurances from God's Word.

Prayers

MORNING PRAYER

*In the morning when you get up, make the sign of the holy
cross and say:*

In the name of ✠ the Father and of the Son and of the Holy Ghost. Amen.

Then, kneeling or standing, repeat the Creed and the Lord's
Prayer. If you choose you may also say this little prayer:

I thank Thee, my heavenly Father,
through Jesus Christ, Thy dear Son,
that Thou hast kept me this night from all harm and danger;
and I pray Thee that Thou wouldst keep me this day also
from sin and every evil,
that all my doings and life may please Thee.
For into Thy hands I commend myself,
my body and soul, and all things,
Let Thy holy angel be with me
that the wicked Foe may have no power over me. Amen.

After singing a hymn (possibly a hymn on the Ten Commandments)
or whatever your devotion may suggest, you should go to your work
joyfully.

EVENING PRAYER

In the evening when you go to bed, make the sign of the holy
cross and say:

In the name of ✠ the Father and of the Son and of the Holy
    Ghost. Amen.

Then, kneeling or standing, repeat the Creed and the Lord's
Prayer. If you choose you may also say this little prayer:

I thank Thee, my heavenly Father,
through Jesus Christ, Thy dear Son,
that Thou hast graciously kept me this day;
and I pray Thee that Thou wouldst forgive me all my sins
    where I have done wrong
and graciously keep me this night.
For into Thy hands I commend myself,
my body and soul, and all things.
Let Thy holy angel be with me
that the wicked Foe may have no power over me. Amen.

Then go to sleep at once and in good cheer.

BLESSING BEFORE EATING

When children and the whole household gather at the table, they
should reverently fold their hands and say:

The eyes of all look to Thee, O Lord,
and Thou givest them their food in due season.
Thou openest Thy hand; Thou satisfiest the desire of every
    living thing.

*Then the Lord's Prayer should be said and afterwards this
prayer:*
Lord God, heavenly Father, bless us
and these Thy gifts which we receive from Thy bountiful goodness,
through Jesus Christ our Lord. Amen.

THANKSGIVING AFTER EATING

*Likewise after eating they should fold their hands
reverently and say:*
O give thanks to the Lord, for He is good,
for His steadfast love endures forever.
He gives to the beasts their food and to the young ravens
    which cry.
His delight is not in the strength of the horse, nor His
    pleasure in the legs of a man;
but the Lord takes pleasure in those who fear Him, in those
    who hope in His steadfast love.

Then the Lord's Prayer should be said and afterwards this prayer:
We give Thee thanks, Lord God, our Father, for all Thy benefits,
through Jesus Christ our Lord, who lives and reigns forever. Amen.

The Practice of Confession and Absolution

The baptized child of God lives in repentance and faith as he responds to the Word of God in his life. Daily the Word of God shows him the mercy of God over against his sinful and needy condition. As he lays the misery of his sin and weakness before God, in faith the child of God trusts that God will forgive him for the sake of Jesus Christ.

When a Christian confesses his sin to God, he may do this before a fellow Christian (especially if he has sinned against him), and certainly before his pastor. The most important part of such personal confession is the absolution that is spoken to him. This is the Word of God that speaks forgiveness in the mouth of the fellow Christian. The confession is prompted by the promise of forgiveness.

If we say we have no sin, we deceive ourselves, and the truth is not in us. If we confess our sins, He is faithful and just and will forgive our sins and cleanse us from all unrighteousness. If we say we have not sinned, we make Him a liar, and His Word is not in us. 1 John 1:8-10.

God forgives those who confess and believe. He does this through the Word of the Gospel spoken to the sinner.

For growth in grace and knowledge and for the assurance of forgiveness, the child of God uses the special ministry of the pastor, who has been called to care for his soul with the Word of God. In private confession the pastor can offer the instruction and consolation of God's Word to the individual penitent sinner. Private confession should not be *demanded* of anyone. But it is offered to all believers as a means to help them remove the burden of a particular sin and to bring them back into their battle against sin with the sure Word of God.

It should be noted that when a person confesses before his pastor, he is actually not confessing his sin to the pastor but to God. The pastor hears this confession and when he speaks the absolution, it is God who forgives.

Here is a way in which an individual Christian may confess his sin before his pastor.

Individual: I confess before you, and to almighty God, that I am a sinful person, that I have sinned against God in my thoughts, words, and deeds. I make no excuse for my grievous sin. I stand under the judgment of God. There is no help for me except that God would look upon me in grace for Jesus' sake and cover me with His righteousness. My heart is troubled with my sin. Especially am I burdened with the weakness and sin of _____.
I pray God for Christ's sake to forgive me and by His Holy Spirit to give me a new heart.

Pastor: Do you believe that God by grace for Jesus' sake forgives you all your sins?

Individual: Yes, I believe this.

Pastor: Do you believe that through me, a called servant of God, you receive forgiveness of all your sins?

Individual: Yes, I believe this. (Here the person may ask the pastor special questions or tell of special problems for instruction in the Word of God.)

Pastor: Almighty God, our heavenly Father, is merciful and gracious and ready to forgive you all your sins for the sake of His Son Jesus Christ, who suffered and died for you. In His name and by His command I declare that you, being penitent, are absolved and free from all your sins.

For your comfort, your peace, and your encouragement, take the assurance I give you in the name of the Lord Jesus. Believe without doubt that your sins are forgiven in the name of the Father ✠ and of the Son ✠ and of the Holy Spirit ✠ Amen. The peace of the Lord be with you. Amen.

THIS IS THE CHRISTIAN FAITH

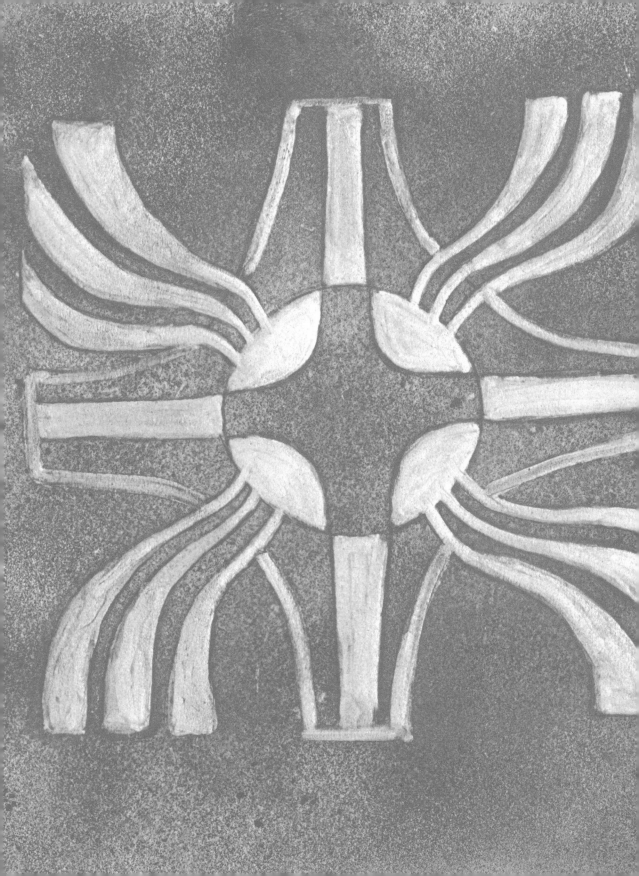

"Let me hear what God the Lord will speak"
Psalm 85:8

Section I: Introduction

1. My Place in God's Plan
2. My God Cares About Me
3. My God Speaks to Me

1

My Place in God's Plan

"In the beginning God . . ."

These are the first words of the Bible. They tell us where we must begin when we think about God. God is greater than our highest thoughts about Him. All life begins with God. Nothing exists that He did not make.

However, God wants us to do more than marvel at Him with open mouths. This great God has a special concern for people. He made them, knows them, and cares about them. That is the heart of the Good News

which God's people believe and talk about. Great God cares about little me!

God not only cares about people. He has a plan for them. He is continually working to bring it about. Thinking about God is not like studying ancient history. God is living and acting for and in people right now.

It sounds like a mystery. It is the mystery of God's love in action. In all the ages of the earth God has revealed His plan and His work. He has spoken directly. He has shown Himself in His actions with individuals and with whole nations. He has recorded His will and His ways in the words of His prophets and apostles. This revelation of God's will and works His people call the Christian faith. As God enters the heart of each individual believer, the Christian confesses: "This Christian faith of the ages is my faith."

THIS IS THE CHRISTIAN FAITH: God Gives Himself to Make People His Own

Christians believe that God has established a covenant with the human race. This means that He has bound Himself to be their God. But He makes no bargains. There is nothing about people that forces God to offer Himself.

As we study the unfolding of God's agreement and plan, we learn that He has made many promises. Peter notes this:

> He has granted to us His precious and very great promises, that through these you may escape from the corruption that is in the world because of passion and become partakers of the divine nature.
>
> *2 Peter 1:4*

The Bible is the story of God keeping His promises. From the earliest chapters of Scripture we learn about God at work making human beings and keeping them His people. God called Abraham and promised to make from him a great and special people. The history of the nation of Israel is the history of God guiding His people. God is still at work with His people. In the midst of all human history, in war and peace, in

politics and science, in joy and tragedy we see God holding fast to His plan to claim a people for Himself. He told Moses:

> ✠ Now therefore, if you will obey My voice and keep My covenant, you shall be My own possession among all peoples; for all the earth is Mine, and you shall be to Me a kingdom of priests and a holy nation.
>
> *Exodus 19:5-6a*

The high point of God's saving actions came in the appearance of His Son. At the birth of the Christ, old Zacharias understood exactly what was happening. He said:

> ✠ Blessed be the Lord God of Israel, for He has visited and redeemed His people.
>
> *Luke 1:68*

Jesus fulfilled God's plan. He put Himself under the Law and kept it perfectly. He became the substitute for all men and bore their guilt and punishment. He was the sacrificial Lamb of God. He tore down the wall that separated man from God. He made it possible for all men to become God's people and to live forever.

After Jesus ascended into heaven, God did not stop working. The Holy Spirit continued to apply Jesus' redeeming work. The Spirit completed giving to the world a trustworthy written account of God's will

and work. The Bible is the written Word of God because:

Men moved by the Holy Spirit spoke from God. *2 Peter 1:21b*

Then began the task of building the church. Spirit-moved people began to speak the good news of God's love to others. Through the proclaiming of the good news the Holy Spirit moved into the hearts of more and more people. Century after century God has been at work building His church. In faith each believer becomes a child of God and a part of the whole "people of God," as Paul points out:

✠ Now you are the body of Christ and individually members of it.
1 Corinthians 12:27

The building goes on. Christians keep telling the good news as God has revealed it. The Holy Spirit works in the Sacrament of Holy Baptism. In the Sacrament of the Lord's Supper God keeps moving into the lives of His people. The eternal God brings Himself to sinful people. He makes them His own. Until the end of this world age, God will go right on keeping His promises and building the church.

This is the plan. This is the broad outline. The details will unfold for us as we move along in this catechism.

THE CHRISTIAN BELIEVES: I Am God's Child in His Plan and Work

Who am I?
I am a creature of this world. I am more than that; I am a child of God. I belong to the vast throng of "the people of God." My life now and to all eternity is bound up with God and His people.

Prayer Thought—

I ask the Holy Spirit to open my heart as
I begin to read and study in God's Word
the details of His plan and actions.

Baptized into Thy name most holy,
O Father, Son, and Holy Ghost,
I claim a place, though weak and lowly,
Among Thy seed, Thy chosen host.
Buried with Christ and dead to sin,
Thy Spirit now shall live within.

My loving Father, Thou dost take me
To be henceforth Thy child and heir;
My faithful Savior, Thou dost make me
The fruit of all Thy sorrows share;
Thou, Holy Ghost, wilt comfort me
When darkest clouds around I see.

Hymn 298, stanzas 1 and 2

33

2

My God Cares About Me

Who is it?

That is my first response when I'm told that I am wanted on the telephone. I almost fly to the telephone if the caller is one I'm anxious to hear. On the other hand, my feet drag if I must talk with someone from whom I would rather not hear.

As I open the pages of this catechism, I know it will have much to say to me. Am I anxious to hear the messages? Who will be speaking to me? Is the author one who doesn't know me and whose name means nothing to me? Is it Martin Luther, a great man of God, who died more than 400 years ago?

The message of this book comes from God. The author and Martin Luther are simply passing on God's messages. I am anxious to hear what God says because I believe—

My God cares about me. God's people have learned that in many ways. The prophet Elijah learned it when he challenged the prophets of Baal. Elijah built an altar; so did the prophets of Baal. Then they prayed to see whose god would send fire to the altar. Baal could not hear or help. No fire came from him. The true God heard Elijah. He cared about His prophet. He showed His care by sending fire to Elijah's altar. With Elijah and God's followers of all ages I believe that my God knows and cares about me.

THIS IS THE CHRISTIAN FAITH: **God Cares for His Believers**

What do we Christians believe about God that makes us so sure He cares?

We remember the great things God has done and still does for all people.

He cares for men because He *created* them. By "men" we mean all human beings. The fact that there are human beings was God's idea.

✠ Then the Lord God formed man of dust from the ground and breathed into his nostrils the breath of life, and man became a living being.
Genesis 2:7

34

Because God cared for men, He redeemed them. God made men perfectly good. But they soon disobeyed God and changed themselves into sinful creatures. God was ready and able to help them. He did not refuse to pay even the highest price.

⊠ He who did not spare His own Son but gave Him up for us all.
Romans 8:32a

Because God cares for men, He uses His divine love to *call them and hold them in faith,* even when they wander from Him.

⊠ By God's power [you] are guarded through faith for a salvation ready to be revealed in the last time.
1 Peter 1:5

35

THE CHRISTIAN BELIEVES: My God Cares for Me

I believe that God cares for *me*. I believe in God's concern for me when I look into my own life to see His care in action.

I believe that God knows my name. He understands my joys and my problems. He is aware of my good points and my weaknesses.

✠ The Lord knows those who are His. *2 Timothy 2:19*

I believe that the blessings of this life come to me from my God. My food and home, parents and friends, health and wealth all come from God. He is a wise and loving Father who knows what to give and what to withhold. I do not know why I receive some gifts and lack others. I believe that my God gives me what I need. Even sickness and pain come from His wisdom and love. I agree with the apostle:

Cast all your anxieties on Him, for He cares about you. *1 Peter 5:7*

I believe that in Baptism God gave me all the benefits earned by His Son. I believe that in this sacrament He adopted me as His child.

I may forget to notice God at work in my life. Yet He never forsakes me. I understand how Jacob felt when God told him:

Behold, I am with you and will keep you wherever you go.

Genesis 28:15a

When my God invites me to learn more about His ways with me, I know He wants to bless me. When He speaks, He should have my attention.

Prayer Thought—

My first prayer in connection with this
catechism is that God will open my eyes
to see and make me eager to learn.
I will be learning about His words and
His will and His actions for me and all
men. I ask Him to open my eyes and ears
to learn well.

Speak, O Lord, Thy servant heareth,
To Thy Word I now give heed;
Life and spirit Thy Word beareth,
All Thy Word is true indeed.

Death's dread power in me is rife;
Jesus, may Thy Word of Life
Fill my soul with love's strong fervor
That I cling to Thee forever.

Hymn 296, stanza 1

3

My God Speaks to Me

Let God speak to me, and I will listen on my knees.
Many people would say that and in the same breath deny that God can speak to them. They go on living as if God were imprisoned in another universe. They think He is unable or unwilling to get in touch with men on earth. As we think about our relationship to God, it is important to know about His speaking to us. This catechism is written in the faith that the God who cares about us also makes Himself known to us.

THIS IS THE CHRISTIAN FAITH: God Makes Himself Known to Us

As soon as we read that statement, we want to know how God talks to men.

The record of God's speaking includes several ways. To Adam and Eve in Eden God's voice came *directly*. To Moses He spoke as a voice out of a *burning bush*. To the Egyptian Pharaoh He spoke through *the voices and words of Moses and Aaron*. He also spoke to the Egyptians through *the 10 plagues*. To some He spoke in *visions* and to others in *dreams*. To Mary, to Joseph, and to the women at the tomb of Jesus, He spoke through *angels*.

The Bible records that at times God spoke clearly *in events in nature*. At other times He spoke *in the affairs of men*. No judge ever spoke more sternly than God when He sent the Flood to destroy all but eight people. The nation of Judah was clearly convicted of its faults when God acted. He used the Babylonians to destroy Judah's cities and enslave the people. In such events He got His message across to the most reluctant hearers.

Sometimes just God's goodness in granting gifts to men has been a message to them, as St. Paul told the people at Lystra:

> He did not leave Himself without witness, for He did good and gave you from heaven rains and fruitful seasons. *Acts 14:17a*

In the writings of the holy Bible God spoke and continues to speak to men. God chose men called prophets in the Old Testament and apostles and evangelists in the New Testament to write the various parts of the Bible. No one can describe how God did it, but somehow He guided these men as they wrote. We say that God inspired them to write, and so the Bible is God's Word. This is how Peter tells about God speaking:

> No prophecy ever came by the impulse of man, but men moved by the Holy Spirit spoke from God. *2 Peter 1:21*

The most important way in which God has spoken and continues to speak to men is *through His Son, Jesus Christ.*

> In many and various ways God spoke of old to our fathers by the prophets, but in these last days He has spoken to us by a Son. *Hebrews 1:1-2*

All that Jesus did and said is God's Word. His words and actions tell us what God is like. He tells us what God wants. He explains what men are like and what God does for them. His words and actions sometimes spell out God's hatred of evil. At other times He speaks or acts out God's amazing patience and mercy. Especially in that awful hour when God's Son died on a cross, God spoke and underlined every word. "Look how evil you are, and see what you deserve," He said. Yet equally clear was His precious message, "See how much I love you. This I do to rescue you."

THE CHRISTIAN BELIEVES: My God
                              Speaks to Me

I am impressed to know that God has thundered at nations and has come to some men in dreams. Still, I want the confidence that He speaks to *me*.

Thank God, none of His messages to men, which He has wanted me to know, have been lost. In the Bible, men of God recorded God's Word. They did not leave out a single word or action of Jesus that I need to know. They wrote of God's power in creation. They wrote down God's will for human conduct. They proclaimed God's judgment against sin. They reported His mercy in promising a Savior. They told of His dealings with people. They explained God's plan for men to live forever. They passed on His promises to answer prayer.

True, the record was made in the Hebrew and Greek languages, but

God has seen to it that dedicated men have collected and translated His messages for me. The Bible is a gift of God to me.

God speaks to me when I read and study what He has said and done. He speaks when I think about my Savior's life and death and rising again. He speaks when I read the Bible. He speaks when the pastor preaches about Him. He speaks in hymns. He speaks when my family conducts devotions. He speaks in tracts and Christian books. He speaks when I see a crucifix and remember that Jesus died for me. He speaks when my friend talks about Him. In many ways God the Holy Spirit makes it possible for me to hear from my God. Jesus promised:

✠ When the Spirit of truth comes, He will guide you into all the truth.

John 16:13a

As a Christian I am confident that my God, who cares about me, also speaks to me. He makes me ready to hear Him.

Prayer Thought—

> In my prayer I need not plead with God
> to speak to me. He is eager to do so.
> Rather, I need His help so that I may be
> ready to hear and to heed His voice.

> Lord, open Thou my heart to hear
> And through Thy Word to me draw near;
> Let me Thy Word e'er pure retain,
> Let me Thy child and heir remain.

Hymn 5, stanza 1

41

"I will run in the way of Thy commandments"
Psalm 119:32

Section II: The Ten Commandments

4. **My God Has Revealed His Law**
5. **He Is the Lord, My God**
6. **I Believe in the Lord, My God**
7. **The First Commandment**
8. **The Second Commandment**
9. **The Third Commandment**
10. **The Fourth Commandment**
11. **The Fifth Commandment**
12. **The Sixth Commandment**
13. **The Seventh Commandment**
14. **The Eighth Commandment**
15. **The Ninth and Tenth Commandments**
16. **The Conclusion of the Commandments**
17. **Gladly Do What He Commands**
18. **Law and Gospel**
19. **Proclaiming Law and Gospel**

My God Has Revealed His Law

Fences and laws are our friends!

Those fences along a mountain road are not meant to keep us from enjoying the ride. They mark the path of safety and warn of danger. Beyond them lies injury or death. Traffic lights may seem to slow us. They really permit us to move more surely.

Laws which control our actions are our friends. Man-made laws are helpful. The law of God is a blessing from His wisdom. God's people have always been concerned about studying, understanding, and following God's law.

THIS IS THE CHRISTIAN FAITH: God Gave His Law for Human Good

When God created men, He wrote His law into their hearts. Adam and Eve knew God's will without asking. They needed no catechism. They knew what God wanted them to do, and they were eager to do it. Moreover, they were able to do all that God wanted. Pleasing God, they were happy.

When these first people disobeyed God, several hurtful things happened to them. They were no longer perfect. They lost their happy relationship with God. They no longer clearly knew His will. God's law in their hearts was blurred. Even though they still knew some of it, they could no longer live according to it. This is the condition of people today. They have a hazy knowledge of God's law and cannot keep it.

> ✠ When Gentiles, who have not the [written] Law, do by nature what the Law requires, they are a law to themselves, even though they do not have the Law. They show that what the Law requires is written in their hearts. *Romans 2:14-15a*

> ✠ Surely there is not a righteous man on earth who does good and never sins. *Ecclesiastes 7:20*

God now chose a special people; He began with Abraham, promising to make him the father of a holy nation. Abraham's descendants were called the Israelites. God made a covenant with Israel. He told Moses to tell the people:

> Now therefore, if you will obey My voice and keep My covenant, you shall be My own possession among all peoples; for all the earth is Mine, and you shall be to Me a kingdom of priests and a holy nation. *Exodus 19:5-6a*

He made the people of Israel "holy," which means "set apart." Through them and their lives God would reveal Himself and His purpose to all nations. Israel was to trust God and obey Him, and God would keep them as His own people.

God gave His law to Israel so that they might know how they were to represent Him to all nations. His commandments showed them how to serve Him by living their lives as people apart from the unbelievers. His laws (ceremonial) directed the kind of sacrifices they were to offer. Some laws directed them in their political affairs. The Ten Commandments are a summary of the moral law.

Although God first gave the Ten Commandments to His people

45

of the old covenant days, our Lord Jesus taught that God's law still governs men today. Jesus summarized the Law in two parts. The first part, or First Table, is:

> "You shall love the Lord your God with all your heart and with all your soul and with all your mind." *Matthew 22:37*

The second part, or Second Table, reads:

> "You shall love your neighbor as yourself." *Matthew 22:39*

The key word in our Lord's summary statements of the Law is *love*. Jesus Christ came to call a new covenant people. By His work sinful man can become holy or set apart. When man accepts Jesus Christ as Savior, God's Spirit lives within him, enabling him to be obedient to God's law in love. The new man in Christ, by the power of the Gospel, lives under God's law.

But this does not remove the force of God's law. God's law still judges all men in their rebellion against God. God's law shows man that his own efforts to be righteous always fail completely. God's law tells man the awful truth of his damnation.

> ✠ For no human being will be justified in His sight by works of the Law, since through the Law comes knowledge of sin. *Romans 3:20*

It is the Gospel of Jesus Christ that moves the sinner to repent. The Gospel gives him the power to live his life as a child of God's new covenant of grace. The psalmist describes God's Word as it guides and empowers the new man.

> Thy Word is a lamp to my feet and a light to my path. *Psalm 119:105*

THE CHRISTIAN BELIEVES: My God's Law Is for Me

God's law is God's Word too. I need God's law, for it shows me my sinfulness. It shows me how often I try to please God by my own righteousness. It keeps reminding me that I can bring nothing to God's throne to avoid condemnation.

God's law is a blessing for me. I have powerful enemies who want me to fail and die. Satan is like a roaring lion. He has many helpers who obey him in rebelling against God. My old Adam within me is also my enemy. God's law condemns me when I listen to them.

Without God's law I would not hear the Gospel. In Jesus is my only hope and life. Jesus Christ alone kept the Law and suffered the curse of it. By His power and grace I can live as one of God's holy people, revealing God's love for all men.

Prayer Thought—

I ask God to use His law to make me
humble. I praise God for His law, which
brings order into our world. I ask God
for His mercy in Christ to forgive me
all my sin. I ask Him for His Holy Spirit
to enable me to live as His child.

The law of God is good and wise
And sets His will before our eyes,
Shows us the way of righteousness,
And dooms to death when we transgress.

Its light of holiness imparts
The knowledge of our sinful hearts
That we may see our lost estate
And seek deliverance ere too late.

Hymn 295, stanzas 1 and 2

5

He Is the Lord, My God

Who is this God who is so interested in human beings? What is He like? The answers to these questions will help us when we look more closely into His Word.

If these questions mean that we want to *understand* God, the only answer is that it can't be done. No one can understand God. We *believe* in God. Since we hardly understand ourselves, it is not surprising that we cannot understand God. As He calls us to trust Him, God does tell us what all we can know about Him.

THIS IS THE CHRISTIAN FAITH: The Lord Is a God of Splendor

God is a real person. He is not just an idea. When Moses asked Him what His name was, God said, "Call Me I AM." The gods of the heathen exist only in the minds of those who worship them. Of them the apostle Paul says:

> We know that an idol has no real existence and that there is no God but one. *1 Corinthians 8:4*

Our God exists and does things.

✳ Our God is in the heavens; He does whatever He pleases. *Psalm 115:3*

Our God is a spirit, that is, a person without a body. Because we cannot understand this, God helps us by talking about Himself in human terms. Sometimes the Bible speaks of God as though He were a human being. It speaks of His hand, arm, eye, finger, or face. He really has none of these. Such words help us to see what God does. In heaven we shall "see Him as He is." (1 John 3:2)

With the eye of faith we see God's "footprints." The unbeliever sees a tree. The believer sees God's wisdom and power in the tree. The unbeliever takes his food for granted. The child of God believes that God has been at work to provide food for him. Job expresses the faith of God's people that God is invisibly present in our lives:

> Lo, He passes by me, and I see Him not; He moves on, but I do not perceive Him.
>
> *Job 9:11*

Our God is the Maker of all things, but no one made Him. He existed before all things and is separate from all things. God "has life in Himself" (John 5:26), while everything else owes its existence to Him. Paul believed:

> ✠ In Him we live and move and have our being. *Acts 17:28a*

Trying to describe God is like trying to put a rainbow into a matchbox. Neither our minds nor our words can fully contain Him. However, He does describe Himself that we may be led to praise Him. In the words of the Bible, in His wondrous acts, and in His Son Jesus Christ He shows His qualities.

> No one has ever seen God; the only Son, who is in the bosom of the Father, He has made Him known.
>
> *John 1:18*

Here are some words that help us when we try to describe God.

> God is *eternal.* He has no beginning or ending. "From everlasting to everlasting Thou art God."
>
> *Psalm 90:2*

> God is *all-powerful.* "For with God nothing will be impossible."
>
> *Luke 1:37*

> ✠ God is *all-knowing.* "The eyes of the Lord are in every place, keeping watch on the evil and the good."
>
> *Proverbs 15:3*

> God *never changes.* "For I the Lord do not change." *Malachi 3:6a*

> God is *holy.* He is set apart from all evil. "Who is like Thee . . . majestic in holiness?"
>
> *Exodus 15:11*

> God is *wise.* "O the depth of the riches and wisdom and knowledge of God!"
>
> *Romans 11:33a*

The apostle John has added to the list the most important of all the words that describe our God:

> God is love. *1 John 4:8b*

God is not merely loving, but He *is* love. He acted out that love especially in giving His Son as a sacrifice on the cross. Jesus on the cross is a way of saying what our God is like. Without this love in Christ, all other descriptions of God might only frighten us. Thanks to God, His Son died for us. By that act He put us into connection with all God's power and glory.

THE CHRISTIAN BELIEVES: The Lord Is My God

I may visit an electric power plant and marvel at it. Its huge dynamos and crackling power may make me feel small and helpless in comparison. However, when I snap on my bedroom light, I know that the power plant is meant to help me in my life.

Likewise, I stand in awe before the mystery and majesty of God. I believe, however, that His power and goodness and love are for me. I rely on His power for every breath I take. I rely on His wisdom to guide my life according to His will. He is all-knowing and present everywhere. Therefore He is present with me and knows me. He wants me to be set apart from evil. His love in Christ is poured out for me. He passes through each day of my life, even if I cannot see Him. Truly, He is the Lord, *my* God.

Prayer Thought—

Adoration is a much-neglected part of prayer. To adore God means to remember His greatness. It includes telling God how we appreciate His majesty. To adore means to tell God of our wonder that such a great God is *our* God. The thoughts of this lesson lead me to adore God.

All glory be to God alone,
Forevermore the Highest One,
Who doth our sinful race befriend
And grace and peace to us extend.
Among mankind may His good will
All hearts with deep thanksgiving fill.

Hymn 238, stanza 1

51

לא תרצח   לא יהיה

לא תנאף   לא תעשה

לא תגנב   לא תשא

לא תענה   זכור את

לא תחמד   כבד את

6

I Believe in the Lord, My God

When God gave the Ten Commandments, He did not begin by telling the people what to do and what not to do. He began by saying, "I am the Lord, your God, who brought you out of the land of Egypt, out of the house of bondage."

The Law would have no meaning for them until they *believed* in their God and what He had promised and done for them. He was the Lord who had made a covenant with them.

This applies to *us* too. We must realize that the commandments require that we believe in God. They were given by One who calls Himself our God and invites us to believe it. We must talk about believing in God before we can talk about doing His will.

THIS IS THE CHRISTIAN FAITH: We Believe
in the Triune God

God invites us to believe in Him. To believe in God, we must know about Him. Knowledge, however, is not yet faith. To believe in God means to trust in Him. A believer is sure that God can and does keep His promises.

People must believe in a surgeon. If they believe, they will permit the surgeon to operate on them. They trust that the surgeon will help them. That is an example of faith in a person. In a much greater way Christians trust their God.

Faith is not a good work. Man cannot take credit for knowing and trusting in God. Man cannot be proud of his loyalties to God's Word. Faith is God's act by which a sinner turns to God and trusts His promises completely. God makes this sinner firm and trustworthy in his belief. Faith is the right relationship with God. The writer to the Hebrews says:

> Without faith it is impossible to please Him. *Hebrews 11:6*
>
> Now faith is the assurance of things hoped for, the conviction of things not seen.   *Hebrews 11:1*

God invites us to believe that He makes promises to us and keeps them. He reminded Israel that He had kept His promise to them. He had promised to make that multitude of slaves into a great nation and to give them a homeland. To such people of promise He gave His laws. They knew that the commands came from a gracious God of promise.

The Law was not given to keep them from enjoying life. It was God's way of governing His people. It gave them an opportunity to show their joy and gratitude to God, who keeps His promises. Their holy life would help reveal the true God to the heathen nations. "I will be your God," said the Lord, "and you shall be My people." Such a God could mean only good when He gave them His law.

When we believe, we have that relationship to God. He is our God. We are His people because He accepts us in Baptism and in Christ adopts us into His family. The Bible points out that believers today are the people of God when it says:

> I will put My laws into their minds and write them on their hearts, and I will be their God, and they shall be My people. *Hebrews 8:10b*

To understand how God works for us, it is helpful to know that God's people refer to Him as the triune God. There is only one true God. He reveals Himself as three Persons: Father, Son, and Holy Spirit. We speak

53

of Him as triune (three-one) and as the Trinity (three-oneness). We do not understand this. We simply take God's Word for it. That is how He speaks of Himself in the Bible.

Knowing the Trinity helps in this way: we can more easily appreciate God's work for us. God in three Persons works for us. The Scriptures ascribe to each a special work. The Father is chiefly known for the work of creation, taking care of us, and sending His Son as our Savior. The Son is chiefly known as our Redeemer. He shed His blood to pay the cost of making us God's children. His sacrifice takes away our sins. The Holy Spirit brings us to faith and keeps us in faith. He enables us to do what God wants. We will study each Person in detail later. Here we want to understand that the God who gives the commandments has done great things to make us His children.

THE CHRISTIAN BELIEVES: The Triune God Calls Me to Faith

God's first word to me is a call for me personally to believe in Him. He tells me: "I am the Lord, *your* God. I claim *you* as Mine. I made *you*. I redeemed *you*. I adopted *you* into My family." As I study the Ten Commandments, I will realize that God is speaking to me.

Prayer Thought —

Trusting in the true God, I can pray to
Him with confidence.

The apostle wrote:

✠ But let him ask in faith, with no doubting, for he who doubts is like a wave of the sea that is driven and tossed by the wind. *James 1:6*

My prayers, therefore, will include requests
that God will help me to believe in Him.
I need His help to conquer my doubts
about Him and His goodness.

We all believe in one true God,
Father, Son, and Holy Ghost,
Ever-present Help in need,
Praised by all the heavenly host,
By whose mighty power alone
All is made and wrought and done.

We all believe in Jesus Christ,
Son of God and Mary's Son,
Who descended from His throne
And for us salvation won;
By whose cross and death are we
Rescued from all misery.

We all confess the Holy Ghost,
Who from both fore'er proceeds;
Who upholds and comforts us
In all trials, fears, and needs.
Blest and Holy Trinity,
Praise forever be to Thee!

Hymn 252, stanzas 1, 2, and 3

7

The First Commandment

To give God some kind of place in our busy lives is not difficult. In the First Commandment, however, God demands not only *a* place but the *first* place.

This makes sense only when we believe that we belong to God. He claims us because He created us. He claims us because He has made us His children by Baptism.

God's people have discovered that living according to the First Commandment, even imperfectly, makes changes in one's life. This commandment is basic to all the rest. Dr. Martin Luther has pointed out that we can keep the others only as we live according to the *First Commandment*.

You shall have no other gods.

What does this mean for us?
We are to fear, love, and trust God above anything else.

THIS IS THE CHRISTIAN FAITH: God Must Have First Place

The Christian faith and Christian living must start with God. That is why the commandments begin with God. When we confess the Apostles' Creed, the same note is sounded. In the Creed we begin by saying, "I believe in God." In the Lord's Prayer we begin with the same thought. The opening words are "Our Father who art in heaven." God comes first.

Giving God first place in our lives means that we are to *fear* Him. We are not to be afraid of God. This fear is a trembling adoration of the Holy God. We show respect for His will. We stand in awe of Him and His holiness, according to the holy writer:

> Therefore let us be grateful for receiving a kingdom that cannot be shaken, and thus let us offer to God acceptable worship, with reverence and awe; for our God is a consuming fire. *Hebrews 12:28-29*

Giving God first place in our lives means that we are to *love* Him. Such love will lead us to please Him at any cost. Abraham is an example. Because he loved God, he was ready to sacrifice his own son (Genesis 22). God expects just that kind of love.

> ✠ He who loves father or mother more than Me is not worthy of Me, and he who loves son or daughter more than Me is not worthy of Me.
> *Matthew 10:37*

Such love does not flow naturally from us, but it is the result of what God does for us.

> ✠ We love because He first loved us. *1 John 4:19*

Giving God first place in our lives means *trusting* Him. We are to believe firmly that God cares for us in the best way and that He will never forsake us. David is an example of such trusting action. Armed with his trust in God, he strode into battle against Goliath (1 Samuel 17). He believed what he later wrote in a psalm:

> ✠ Commit your way to the Lord; trust in Him, and He will act. *Psalm 37:5*

It is not enough, however, just to fear and love and trust God. We must fear, love, and trust Him *above anything or anyone else*. Whenever we put any thing or any person before God in our lives, we are having another god. This is called idolatry.

There are many ways to break this commandment. Some people actually make gods of wood or stone and worship them. Others think of trees, rivers, or animals as their gods. Some turn away from the true God and imagine a god of their own. This coarser kind of idolatry is easy to recognize.

Another kind of idolatry is not as easy to recognize. Anything that is put ahead of God becomes an idol. It is a sin to put oneself ahead of God. Money or pleasure or loved ones — all of these are idols if we think more of them than we do of God.

Peter feared men more than God and denied Jesus. A rich young ruler loved money more than God and turned away from Jesus. Goliath trusted in his own strength and laughed at David's God. God will permit *no* other gods.

✠ I am the Lord, that is My name; My glory I give to no other, nor My praise to graven images.
Isaiah 42:8

THE CHRISTIAN BELIEVES: God Must Be First in My Life

I believe that God is present with me always. I don't want to offend Him with my sin.

I believe that God loves me and has shown His love in more ways than I can count. My life is to show my love to Him.

I believe that God is both able and willing to keep His promises, so that I am to trust Him completely.

58

In my life I have put other things ahead of God. I do not bow to statues, but I do crowd God out of my life. Pleasures and worldly interests often slide into first place. Even my worries show that I do not always trust God. So of myself I despair of keeping this commandment.

My hope is in God. Jesus kept this commandment perfectly. His life is a story of perfect fear and love and trust in His heavenly Father. He is not only my example. He kept all the commandments for me. He died to wash away my sins against this and all other commandments.

Prayer Thought—

Each commandment drives me to confess my sin and admit my guilt. It is well to do this directly to God in prayer. Each commandment makes me cry for forgiveness. Knowing that Jesus has saved me from my sin calls for words of gratitude. I may close my prayer by asking for new strength to fear, love, and trust in my God.

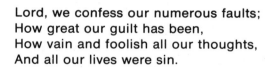

Lord, we confess our numerous faults;
How great our guilt has been,
How vain and foolish all our thoughts,
And all our lives were sin.

'Tis from the mercy of our God
That all our hopes begin;
'Tis by the water and the blood
Our souls are washed from sin.

Hymn 382, stanzas 1 and 4

59

8

The Second Commandment

Do we really know God's name?
We know several names for God. Among them are Lord, God, Christ, Jesus, Father, the Almighty, Holy Spirit, and others. Each name tells us something about our God. Most of the names tell us what God does. In its fullest sense, God's name includes everything by which He makes Himself known. This is why Jesus, in praying to His Father, says:

> ✠ I have manifested *Thy name* to the men whom Thou gavest Me out of the world.
> *John 17:6a*

Jesus had not told them only one name for God. He had taught them all they were to know about God. All of this teaching He referred to as "manifesting God's name."

We must keep this definition in mind as we think about the *Second Commandment*. There are right and wrong ways of using God's name.

You shall not take the name of the Lord your God in vain.

What does this mean for us?
We are to fear and love God so that we do not use His name superstitiously, or use it to curse, swear, lie, or deceive, but call on Him in prayer, praise, and thanksgiving.

THIS IS THE CHRISTIAN FAITH: God's Name Is Holy to His People

When we say that God's name is holy, we mean also that God sets it apart from all evil. This we are to remember when we use it. God's name is to be used with care and reverence. It is like an expensive tool that a man uses in his work. He carefully protects it against abuse. So God gives us His name to bless us and bring us salvation.

> In every place where I cause My name to be remembered I will come to you and bless you.
> *Exodus 20:24b*

Everyone who calls upon the name of the Lord will be saved.

Romans 10:13

We therefore love and fear our God and believe that His name is a precious gift. God firmly commands us to avoid thoughtless and evil use of His name:

✠ The Lord will not hold him guiltless who takes His name in vain.

Exodus 20:7b

It is a misuse of God's name to *curse*. This means to call down God's anger upon ourselves or others or to speak evil of God. A curse is a sinful use of God's name, whether it is really intended as such or only spoken in thoughtless anger. Among the people of Israel it was considered worthy of death. Their law said:

✠ Whoever curses his God shall bear his sin. *Leviticus 24:15*

It is a misuse of God's name to *swear*. Only when the glory of God or the need of a fellowman demand it (as in court) may we use God's name in speaking an oath.

It is a misuse of God's name to try to *gain knowledge of the future by it.* God forbids fortune-telling, superstitions, and good luck charms; those who try to bring messages from the dead are deceivers. When all this is done in God's name, it is especially wicked. God says:

> Behold, I am against the prophets . . . who use their tongues and say, "Says the Lord."
> *Jeremiah 23:31*

It is a misuse of God's name to *lie or deceive by it.* We are not to use His name to cover up a lie, to get people to believe false religious teachings, or to make people think we are devoted to God when we are not.

Our respect and love for God lead us to use His name properly.

We use His name rightly in prayer. It is proper to say "God" or "Jesus" in prayer. We may use any of God's names in prayer. Trusting His promises and His wisdom, we believe:

> ✠ The Lord is near to all who call upon Him, to all who call upon Him in truth.
> *Psalm 145:18*

We use His name rightly in *praise and thanksgiving.* God wants us to tell Him and others what we think of His goodness. This is one of His reasons for choosing us as His own people.

> But you are a chosen race, a royal priesthood, a holy nation, God's own people, that you may declare the wonderful deeds of Him who called you out of darkness into His marvelous light.
> *1 Peter 2:9*

An interesting name sometimes given to the Book of Psalms is "The Praises of Israel." In it we find hundreds of prayers of thanksgiving which we may use as our own. God's people agree that—

> ✠ It is good to give thanks to the Lord, to sing praises to Thy name, O Most High; to declare Thy steadfast love in the morning and Thy faithfulness by night.
> *Psalm 92:1-2*

THE CHRISTIAN BELIEVES: I Am Responsible for the Holiness of God's Name in My Life

Many people lightly misuse God's name in foul speech and oaths and curses. I am not to follow this example. I am a child of God. My heart and mind and lips belong to Him. They are meant for His praise.

Jesus always treated God's name as a precious jewel. He is my example. Moreover, I trust His grace and mercy to forgive my sins against this commandment. He will help me to pray, to praise, and to give thanks to God.

Prayer Thought—

> I do well to study the Psalms to find beautiful prayers that I may include among my own prayers. Especially for thanksgiving prayers I may use words from Psalms 103, 104, 111, and many others.

> By idle word and speech profane
> Take not My holy name in vain,
> And praise but that as good and true
> Which I Myself say and do.
> Have mercy, Lord!
>
> *Hymn 287, stanza 3*

9

The Third Commandment

Don't forget to eat!

That commandment is not necessary except for people who are ill and have lost their appetites. For the nourishing of our spiritual life, however, we do need such a commandment. Sin is a sickness that spoils our appetites for the food our souls must have. Besides, Satan tricks us into believing that only our bodies are important. He tried to convince even Jesus that only food for the body is important. Our Lord threw his lie back at him, saying:

> It is written, "Man shall not live by bread alone, but by every word that proceeds from the mouth of God." *Matthew 4:4*

64

God has given the *Third Commandment* to help His people remember the need for feeding on His Word.

Remember the Sabbath Day, to keep it holy.

What does this mean for us?

We are to fear and love God so that we do not neglect His Word and the preaching of it, but regard it as holy and gladly hear and learn it.

THIS IS THE CHRISTIAN FAITH: Christian Life Must Be Nourished by God's Word

In Old Testament times God guided His people Israel as if they were children. He told them in detail how they were to worship. He even told them how to erect their worship building. The Sabbath was God's special arrangement to help Israel live as His people. On the seventh day of each week they rested from their usual work and gave special attention to the worship of God.

In the Old Testament God gave His people special rules that pointed forward to the Messiah. With the coming of the Messiah these special regulations were fulfilled. Therefore the Sabbath law is not binding on us, as Paul writes:

> ✠ Therefore let no one pass judgment on you in questions of food and drink or with regard to a festival or a new moon or a sabbath. These are only a shadow of what is to come; but the substance belongs to Christ. *Colossians 2:16-17*

Jesus Himself puts the Sabbath in its place:

> The Sabbath was made for man, not man for the Sabbath; so the Son of Man is Lord even of the Sabbath. *Mark 2:27-28*

God's people have kept the real purpose of sabbaths and holy days. They have rejoiced to gather to hear His Word. They followed the advice:

> . . . not neglecting to meet together, as is the habit of some, but encouraging one another. *Hebrews 10:25a*

In the days of the apostles, Christians chose the first day of the week for worship. They called it the Lord's Day. It has been a weekly reminder of Jesus' rising from the dead on the first day of the week.

Later God's people adopted special days to remember Jesus' birth

(Christmas), when He was revealed as Savior of all (Epiphany), His giving of the Holy Supper (Maundy Thursday), His dying on the cross (Good Friday), and other important events. Thus the Sundays and festivals of the church year have come to be observed as occasions for special worship.

No one has forced God's people to do all this. They freely chose days so that they could hear God's Word and worship Him. Year after year they tell the wonderful story to one another, remembering God's great acts.

However, we use God's Word not only on Sundays and in church. God gives us His Word to use at home or wherever we are. Hearing His Word brings faith to our hearts and nourishes our spiritual lives.

> So faith comes from what is heard, and what is heard comes by the preaching of Christ. *Romans 10:17*
>
> Receive with meekness the implanted Word, which is able to save your souls. *James 1:21b*

Hearing God's Word is not meant to be an unpleasant chore. It is to be done gladly. David knew the blessings of God's Word, and so he sang:

> O Lord, I love the habitation of Thy house and the place where Thy glory dwells. *Psalm 26:8*

We expect a blessing when we gather to hear God's Word:

> Blessed rather are those who hear the Word of God and keep it! *Luke 11:28*
>
> The law of Thy mouth is better to me than thousands of gold and silver pieces. *Psalm 119:72*

**THE CHRISTIAN BELIEVES: I Delight in the
                             Word of the Lord**

There are so many things to do—I cannot hope to do them all. As I plan my time, I decide to do first the things that *must* be done. Other things I may not be able to do at all. The really important things must come first.

Since I belong to God, His Word must be first in my life.

By giving me His Word, God does me a favor. I am to hear His Word gladly, not grudgingly. I believe that He will bless me all my life through the hearing of His Word. Such blessings will be for my spiritual life first. However, God's Word is a blessing even for my earthly life.

66

God has given me pastors and teachers and parents that I may hear and know what the Word means. They are gifts from God. With them I find eternal treasures in what God says to me in His Word.

Prayer Thought—

To be able to go to my church and read
my Bible is a privilege. Not all people
enjoy this privilege. I ought to say a prayer
of gratitude to God for giving us His Word.
I may ask God to help me value this
freedom by using it often.

Lord, open Thou my heart to hear
And through Thy Word to me draw near;
Let me Thy Word e'er pure retain,
Let me Thy child and heir remain.

Hymn 5, stanza 1

10

The Fourth Commandment

✠ And this is His commandment, that we should believe in the name of His Son Jesus Christ and love one another, just as He has commanded us.
1 John 3:23

The two go together!

A Christian loves God because God loves him. But love does not stop there. God's love working in us goes out in all directions to our fellowmen.

God asks us to see other people as He sees them. Of course some people annoy us. We are all sinful. We all need God's forgiving love. That is just the point. God daily forgives us for Jesus' sake. We are to deal with other people as our Father does. He loves them as He loves us. By loving them we show our love to God.

In the last seven commandments God tells us what it means to love our neighbor. He talks first about our closest "neighbors." These are our parents and others in authority over us; they are included in the *Third Commandment*.

Honor your father and your mother.

What does this mean for us?

We are to fear and love God so that we do not despise or anger our parents and others in authority, but respect, obey, love, and serve them.

THIS IS THE CHRISTIAN FAITH: God Is to Be Honored in His Representatives

Christians believe that God is the ruler of this world. They believe that He rules through various kinds of people. Recall that Jesus said to Pilate:

> You would have no power over Me unless it had been given you from
> above. *John 19:11a*

We believe that God gives some of His power to *parents* to rule their children. To respect and obey parents is to respect God. To despise them is to despise God.

✠ Children, obey your parents in everything, for this pleases the Lord.
Colossians 3:20

The Scriptures give many examples of God's anger over disobedient children and His pleasure over the obedient. Jesus set the perfect example. He showed His duty to His heavenly Father in the temple, and He showed love and honor to His earthly parents.

> And He went down with them and came to Nazareth and was obedient to them. *Luke 2:51a*

On the cross, Jesus was at work redeeming a lost world. Yet He took the time to see that His mother was cared for.

The Bible warns us by telling us of Absalom's despising of his father, King David. With equal clearness it pictures Joseph, second in power to the king of Egypt, honoring his aged father.

We believe that God also gives some of His power to *leaders of the government* for ruling the people. The apostle Paul writes even to the people who lived under the corrupt Roman empire:

> ✠ Let every person be subject to the governing authorities. For there is no authority except from God, and those that exist have been instituted by God. *Romans 13:1*

Our President, Governors, Mayors, and all whom God has placed over us today are to be respected and honored. They are not perfect, but they exercise God's power in their offices.

We believe that God also gives some of His power to pastors and leaders in the *church.* As they preach and teach for God, we are to respect and obey them for their work's sake.

> ✠ Obey your leaders and submit to them; for they are keeping watch over your souls, as men who will have to give account.
> *Hebrews 13:17a*

We believe that God wants pupils to respect their *teachers.* Elisha honored his teacher Elijah. He called him his "father."

We believe that God wants people to honor *those for whom they work.* He told servants to be subject to their masters. In honesty we are to do what we are paid to do.

Furthermore, we believe God's *promise* that obedience and respect will bring blessings for this earthly life. In giving the commandment to Moses, God said:

> ✠ Honor your father and your mother, that your days may be long in the land which the Lord your God gives you. *Exodus 20:12*

In the New Testament, Paul repeats the commandment and the promise (Ephesians 6:2-3). He reminds us that obedience will bring harmony between parents and children and between authorities and those under them. Disobedience and disrespect bring unhappiness and trouble.

Most of all, we believe that God's spiritual blessings are passed on by parents to their obedient children. Parents are to care for their children's bodily needs. Spiritual care is even more important. To parents God says:

> ✠ Fathers, do not provoke your children to anger, but bring them up in the discipline and instruction of the Lord. *Ephesians 6:4*

See how Timothy, Paul's co-worker, was blessed by his mother:

> I am reminded of your sincere faith, a faith that dwelt first in your grandmother Lois and your mother Eunice and now, I am sure, dwells in you. *2 Timothy 1:5*

THE CHRISTIAN BELIEVES: I Am to Respect God by My Obedience

It is easier for me to agree with this commandment than to keep it. My pride and desire to have my own way lead me to break it. God wants me to obey this commandment with my parents, my teachers, my pastor, and my government.

I know that God intends to build me up in faith through the guidance of my elders. I must give their work my attention and faithfulness.

I know that God blesses me when I am obedient. When I am rebellious, I bring unhappiness upon myself and others. My flesh is weak. I need God's forgiveness for my breaking of this commandment. I need His help if I am to live as His respectful child.

Prayer Thought—

> I pray that I may remember that parents and others in authority are God's representatives. I pray that my life may honor Him in them. I repent of my past sins against this commandment. I ask for wisdom and strength to follow my God's will.

> Hear us, dear Father, when we pray
> For needed help from day to day
> That as Thy children we may live,
> Whom Thou in Baptism didst receive.
> *Hymn 288, stanza 3*

11

The Fifth Commandment

Must we fear and love God to keep this commandment? Isn't the fear of human punishment enough to keep men from killing?

Human laws might be enough to stop many crimes of murder. God, however, is concerned about much more than actual murder.

People who do not fear and love God may think they have kept this commandment if they have not taken another person's life. "Live and let live," they say.

Our God says, "Live and help live." He places upon His people the task of actively helping others. Just to let others alone is not enough. Yet, to feel that we must help others is not a natural feeling. Christians, however, live by faith in Christ and have a new way of looking at things. A large part of the Christian life is guided by the *Fifth Commandment.*

You shall not kill.

What does this mean for us?
We are to fear and love God so that we do not hurt our neighbor in any way, but help him in all his physical needs.

THIS IS THE CHRISTIAN FAITH: **God's People Are**
Responsible for the
Bodily Welfare of Others

We believe that God alone has the right to take human life. He gives life; He takes it when people die. If a court sentences a person to death, it does so as God's representative. As God's representative a government may also send its citizens to war. Government gives its citizens the right of self-defense. We do not have the right to take our own lives (suicide). God's order is clear:

I kill and I make alive; I wound and I heal. *Deuteronomy 32:39*

✠ Whoever sheds the blood of man, by man shall his blood be shed; for God made man in His own image.   *Genesis 9:6*

We believe that deliberately or carelessly hurting one's own or another person's body is forbidden. Joseph's brothers broke this commandment by selling him as a slave. They also hurt their father by telling him that Joseph was dead. Our fear and love of God move us not to hurt others or cause them sorrow in any way.

Furthermore, *we believe* that God does not want us to hate others.

Ungodly people may scoff and say, "We may hate others so long as we do not actually hurt them." The Scriptures say:

> ✠ Anyone who hates his brother is a murderer, and you know that no murderer has eternal life abiding in him. *1 John 3:15*

Unbelievers are puzzled when we tell them that *we believe* that we do not have the right to "get back" at people who hurt us. Love of God moves us to forgive, as we are forgiven. We let God deal with evildoers.

> ✠ Beloved, never avenge yourselves, but leave it to the wrath of God; for it is written, "Vengeance is mine, I will repay, says the Lord." *Romans 12:19*

We believe that each Christian is appointed by God as a caretaker of other people. Our Savior has given us a wonderful example. We remember His kind deeds reported in the gospels:

> He went about doing good and healing all that were oppressed by the devil. *Acts 10:38*

The fear and love of God in our hearts will show itself in our loving concern for others. As if we were agents of God, He instructs us:

> Do not neglect to do good and to share what you have, for such sacrifices are pleasing to God. *Hebrews 13:16*

Doing good, even to our enemies and without hope of being repaid, is a mark of the Christian, as Jesus said:

> But love your enemies, and do good, and lend, expecting nothing in return, and your reward will be great, and you will be sons of the Most High; for He is kind to the ungrateful and the selfish. Be merciful, even as your Father is merciful. *Luke 6:35-36*

The greatest reward of all for helping others is to know that we are doing God's work. Through His people He sends His loving care to those who need it. Jesus' words have always excited God's people:

> Truly, I say to you, as you did it to one of the least of these My brethren, you did it to Me. *Matthew 25:40*

THE CHRISTIAN BELIEVES: I Am Responsible for Doing Good to Others

Certainly I must avoid killing or hating others. Moreover I am to take an active part in making God's love felt in the lives of other people. I am to look for opportunities to share His love with all whom He places in touch with my life. Calls to give of my money, my time, and my work for people less fortunate than I come to me from God. As His child I will see them as assignments from Him.

My sinful nature bids me to say, "Let other people worry about themselves." But then I remember that my own life has been paid for by the sacrifice of Christ. Indeed, I am not my own. God has made me His own that His goodness toward all men may work through me.

Prayer Thought—

Intercession is the act of praying for the
bodily and spiritual needs *of others.*
I am to look for the needs of others and to
pray for them. Also, I will need God's
urging to help me go with willing hands
to help those for whom I pray.

All are redeemed, both far and wide,
Since Thou, O Lord, for all hast died.
Oh, teach us, whatsoe'er betide,
To love them all in Thee!

In sickness, sorrow, want, or care,
Whate'er it be, 'tis ours to share;
May we, where help is needed, there
Give help as unto Thee!

Hymn 439, stanzas 4 and 5

75

12

The Sixth Commandment

A great river is a force for good. Millions of tons of water flow steadily between the banks, bringing power and life to cities and farms. Under control the river is a power for blessing.

In a flood this peaceful river turns into a destroyer, bringing trouble. Out of control the river is a power for misery.

Men have learned how to restrain many such threatening rivers. Dams may be built across them, and levees may be thrown up along their banks. In time of high water they hold the river in check and prevent it from destroying. Under control again, the river is once more a blessing.

In some ways resembling the river there is a power in the body and mind of every human being. This power is called sex. God put it in man as a blessing; because of sin man misuses this power. And now it may destroy body and soul. Nevertheless, like the river, it can be contained and kept as a force for good. The Holy Spirit protects the blessing of sex in the *Sixth Commandment.*

You shall not commit adultery.

What does this mean for us?
We are to fear and love God so that in matters of sex our words and conduct are pure and honorable, and husband and wife love and respect each other.

THIS IS THE CHRISTIAN FAITH: God Gives and in Christ Controls the Power of Sex

God put the power of sex into human beings when He created them. By sex we mean God's arrangement whereby a man and woman come to love each other, give themselves to each other for the rest of their lives, and have children. This is God's plan that we call marriage and family life. The joining of a man and a woman in marriage for mutual joy and to have children is not a human invention. It is part of God's wise plan. In God's sight, marriage is the lifelong union of one man and one woman. God began it with Adam and Eve.

NOW!
FORBIDDEN LUST!
ADULTS ONLY
POSITIVELY UNCENSORED!
PLUS ON STAGE!
BABY LU!
girls!

> Then the Lord God said, "It is not good that the man should be alone; I will make him a helper fit for him." *Genesis 2:18*

Through sin the power of sex gets out of control. It drives people to all kinds of evil deeds that upset God's plans for human happiness.

There are many ugly words which refer to the abuse of sexual power. "Adultery" is any action by which people use sex for selfish purposes. It includes getting a divorce contrary to God's will—and the sins that lead to it.

Sex is a power that can be turned into wrong channels by evil pictures, books that tell of sex sins, or unclean "jokes."

Satan is a deceiver. In sins of sex he promises pleasure. However, the shattered families and lives of countless numbers of people reveal the terrible, destructive power of the sins of sex. God warns against these sins. He calls us to a pure life.

> ✠ But immorality and all impurity or covetousness must not even be named among you, as is fitting among saints. *Ephesians 5:3*
>
> ✠ For God has not called us for uncleanness but in holiness. *1 Thessalonians 4:7*

We are to be holy in matters of sex; that is, set apart from ungodly abuse of this blessing. But if this power is built into our bodies, *how can we control it?* Men with good intentions have fallen into sins of sex. We cannot always trust our good intentions.

> The spirit indeed is willing, but the flesh is weak. *Mark 14:38b*

This is where the third and controlling force must take over. As dams control a river, so Christ in our hearts by faith controls the power of sex.

This involves *trust.* Trust is relying upon God, who loves us and gave His Son for us. He provides forgiveness. He grants strength to remain pure. We plead for this controlling force as we pray in worship:

> ✠ Create in me a clean heart, O God, and put a new and right spirit within me. *Psalm 51:10*

We need Christ's power at work in our hearts through His Word. Then the power of sex can be controlled. We may use it for the joy of having a home, a husband or wife, and a happy family life.

In a Christian home, father and mother deeply love each other. In such a home the parents and children find real joy. They work and play and worship together. They talk and sing. They show their affection by the way they look at each other and touch each other. In all this God has first place. He makes families. He blesses His people in their families when sex is used as God intended it to be used.

THE CHRISTIAN BELIEVES: Christ Can Keep Me Pure

From the world about me and from thoughts and feelings that come from within me I am tempted to sins of sex. I must be careful what I read and what movies I see. My friends and I must help each other to remain pure in word and deed. Even curiosity can start trouble.

However, I cannot conquer this sin by my own power. I need Christ's help. Since I belong to Him by my baptism, His power is available to me.

Every day, especially in moments of temptation, the Word of God is a strength for me. By God's grace I will remain pure. Then I will be prepared to serve Him also in a happy marriage if that is His eventual will for me. Right now, in my family I can learn and practice how to be a real man or a lovely woman in Christ.

Prayer Thought—

Jesus told His disciples: "Watch and pray that you enter not into temptation." My prayer in connection with this commandment should take to God my own special problems and struggles. I ask the Holy Spirit to help me to victory over sins of sex.

Destroy in me the lust of sin,
From all impureness make me clean.
Oh, grant me power and strength, my God,
To strive against my flesh and blood!

Hymn 398, stanza 2

13

The Seventh Commandment

God is the owner of everything.

He does not really *give* His possessions to anyone. He lets people *use* His things. For His own reasons He permits some people to manage many things. Other people manage few things.

How easy it is to forget this. Even Christians say, "This is my house." What they mean is: "This is God's house. He has placed it in my care."

Because all things belong to God, He cares about what happens to them. He wants people to manage His property wisely. He does not want us to take things He has entrusted to others. That is why He gave the *Seventh Commandment* about earthly possessions.

You shall not steal.

What does this mean for us?

We are to fear and love God so that we do not take our neighbor's money or property, or get them in any dishonest way, but help him to improve and protect his property and means of making a living.

THIS IS THE CHRISTIAN FAITH: God's People Respect What God Gives to Them and Others

How do we receive our share of God's possessions? Some we receive as gifts from other people. Some we earn by working. Some we buy with money we have earned. In every case God is the Giver.

> ✠ Every good endowment and every perfect gift is from above, coming down from the Father of lights . . .   *James 1:17a*

In His wisdom God decides that some people receive more, others less. People compare what they have with what others have. Then some begin to desire what others have. This leads to stealing.

The evil heart of man has invented many ways of getting for self what God has entrusted to others. Man's laws have different names for the various ways of stealing. Robbery means taking things by force. Theft is stealing when others are not looking.

Shoplifters take things from store counters. Storekeepers may charge too much or sell poor goods under false pretense. Dishonest men get people to sign papers they have not read and then cheat them. Bank robbers blast safes open with dynamite. Car thieves drive off with other people's cars.

81

Some people make careless debts and fail to repay. Others cheat the government by lying when they pay taxes. Some waste time or do poor work for their employer. Others take advantage of people who borrow money by charging too high a rate of interest.

Countless human laws have been written to curb all such forms of dishonesty. God forbids it all when He says, "Do not steal."

> ✠ Let the thief no longer steal, but rather let him labor, doing honest work with his hands, so that he may be able to give to those in need.
> *Ephesians 4:28*

Call it what we will, be as clever as we may—even find "legal" ways to steal—God is not deceived by any such trick. As Christians we know that we cannot steal from anyone without stealing from God. All property is really God's.

God's concern about what we do with His possessions does not stop with forbidding stealing. He shows that the Christian faith includes responsibility. This commandment spells out a duty. We are to help our neighbor with earthly possessions.

Is a neighbor hungry or cold? His need is our opportunity to use God's possessions to show His love.

> ✠ Do not neglect to do good and to share what you have, for such sacrifices are pleasing to God.
> *Hebrews 13:16*

Is our neighbor's property in danger by fire, flood, or other loss? The Christian feels responsible for coming to his aid.

> But if any one has the world's goods and sees his brother in need, yet closes his heart against him, how does God's love abide in him?
> *1 John 3:17*

Jesus wants His followers to be concerned about the needs of others. To help others is to help Him. This includes concern for a neighbor's goods as well as his body.

THE CHRISTIAN BELIEVES: God's Will Guides My Attitude Toward My Own and My Neighbor's Goods

Satan whispers lies to me. He tries to convince me that money is the most important thing in the world. If I heed his lies, I will be greedy and selfish. The next step may be some form of stealing.

God's Word speaks to me too. God reminds me that I own nothing. I am to use His gifts according to His will. He owes me nothing, but in mercy He has bound Himself to me. He gave His Son to cleanse me of my sin and make me His child. His love and wisdom grant me what I need.

Some earthly goods I may use for myself. Some I may use as God's representative for others. Some I may use to do God's work. I am a manager, or steward, of God's property.

I believe that God has made me responsible for what He has given others. I am not to envy them. I am not to try to get their possessions for myself. As God's helper I am to help them keep and improve what God has put in their charge.

Of course it is wrong to steal. But furthermore God has given me the privilege of telling others of our salvation through Jesus. How could I ever do this for someone from whom I had stolen? By helping others keep their earthly goods I may win their friendship. Then they may listen when I tell them of Jesus, the precious gift of God.

Prayer Thought—

> I need to pray for God's grace that
> I may use my talents and possessions in
> His service. I am tempted to greed, envy,
> and selfishness every day. I admit to God
> that I am troubled by them. I ask Him for
> strength to fight them. Nothing in this
> world can make me any richer than I am.
> I thank God that I am His child and
> in Christ an heir of all God's riches.

> And let me with all men,
> As far as in me lieth,
> In peace and friendship live.
> And if Thy gift supplieth
> Great wealth and honor fair,
> Then this refuse me not,
> That naught be mingled there
> Of goods unjustly got.

Hymn 395, stanza 5

14

The Eighth Commandment

It is not difficult to find faults in other people.
All human beings are sinful. If we watch any person long enough, we will catch him in sin.

God has not told us to look for faults in other people. He has told His followers to love others in spite of their faults. He loves all people. His love cost Him very much. He gave His Son as a sacrifice to save all people.

Because God sacrificed so much for all people, He is concerned about what happens to them in their daily lives. Among His best earthly gifts to men is a good name. He knows how quickly a good name can be destroyed by wagging tongues. Therefore He has given the *Eighth Commandment,* that judges our unkind words and thoughts about our neighbor and guides us in the way we should speak about him.

You shall not bear false witness against your neighbor.

What does this mean for us?
We are to fear and love God so that we do not betray, slander, or lie about our neighbor, but defend him, speak well of him, and explain his actions in the kindest way.

THIS IS THE CHRISTIAN FAITH: God's People Protect the Neighbor's Good Name

Because Christians fear and love God, they see their fellowmen as God sees them. God forbids bearing false witness because it hurts others.

It is not loving God to *betray* another person. To betray means to tell secret things about someone else. It is a great temptation to reveal secrets. It makes some people feel important to tell about other people's sins. How quickly such secrets leak out and pass from person to person. The Lord tells us what to do when we know about another person's faults:

> ✠ If your brother sins against you, go and tell him his fault between you and him alone.
> *Matthew 18:15a*

As for telling others, Scripture says:

> ✠ He who goes about as a talebearer reveals secrets, but he who is trustworthy in spirit keeps a thing hidden.
> *Proverbs 11:13*

It is not loving God to *slander* or *lie about* our neighbor. A witness in court is under oath. If he lies about someone, he may be punished for perjury. If someone deliberately prints lies about another person in a book or newspaper, he is guilty of libel and deserves to be punished.

There are few laws of man to punish liars. However, God forbids all kinds of lying.

People lie about others for various reasons. Sometimes they want to make the other person appear evil. What they may mean is, "Look how much better I am." Sometimes they try to steal business or friends by lying about others.

85

Sometimes they may even think they are telling the truth. They pass on an evil story without checking it. Later they may be sorry that they were led to spread a lie.

One thing we may be sure of is that love is not the source of lies. St. Paul reminds us of our duty to love our fellowmen when he writes:

> ✠ Therefore, putting away falsehood, let every one speak the truth with his neighbor, for we are members one of another. *Ephesians 4:25*

Loving God leads us to *defending* our neighbor. It is not easy to speak up for someone. It is more popular to join in condemning an absent person. But it is cowardly to talk about someone behind his back. The power of Christ's love gives courage. True bravery means to defend those who cannot defend themselves. This is especially true when they are being attacked with lies and evil words.

Loving God leads us to *speak well* of our neighbor. How good it is to receive a compliment! Everyone hungers to have good things said about him. The person with a loving heart looks for good things in others. Then he talks about the good things he sees. He is not a miser with compliments.

Loving God leads us to *explain our neighbor's actions in the kindest light.* Almost any action can be explained in several ways. Some people regularly choose the least charitable explanation. A man's picture may appear in a newspaper because he gave money to a good cause. Some will hint that he just wanted to get his picture in the paper. Other will suggest that he had a guilty conscience. Some will choose the kindest explanation. They will note that he is a generous man.

In speaking about others, as we often do, let us show the love of God in our hearts.

> ✠ Above all, hold unfailing your love for one another, since love covers a multitude of sins.
> *1 Peter 4:8*

THE CHRISTIAN BELIEVES: I Show My Love of God in Speaking of My Neighbor

I see how I have sinned against this commandment. My ears have itched to hear bad things about others. I have readily passed on gossip. I have been quick to judge others and excuse myself.

I cannot even know all my sins against this commandment. Was my teacher ill-tempered? Or was she really ill? Was that person a snob, as I said? Or was he shy and afraid? Did the grocer try to cheat me? Or did he make an honest mistake? Did my friend really cheat on an examination? Or did my envy of his high mark make me imagine that he did?

My Savior spoke well even of those who nailed Him to the cross. His great love is available also for me. His love for me is my only hope for forgiveness. His great love for me will help me lead the life of Christian love—even with my tongue.

Prayer Thought—

> Sins against this commandment start in my heart. My prayer may ask God for cleansing. What makes me speak evil of others? Is it pride or envy or cowardice? God will hear my prayer for cleansing.

> Jesus, Savior, wash away
> All that has been wrong today;
> Help me every day to be
> Good and gentle, more like Thee.
> *Hymn 653, stanza 2*

15

The Ninth and Tenth Commandments

The last two commandments are different from the others.
In the first eight commandments God tells us what we are to do or not do. At first we may think God now adds to the list. Closer study shows a difference.

The last two commandments lead us to ask: "What kind of person does God want each of us to be?"

Every stream has a source. The sinful actions of men are like a stream. Where do they all begin?

Jesus says that a person who lives without fear and love of God has a wicked heart. From his wicked heart flow wicked deeds.

> ✠ Out of the heart come evil thoughts, murder, adultery, fornication, theft, false witness, slander.   *Matthew 15:19*

People think they can please God by doing more good things than bad things. It surprises them that God considers it sinful to *think* wrong things. Beyond this, it is sinful even to *be* the kind of person who can think or do wrong. All hope of pleasing God by ourselves is destroyed. The *Ninth* and *Tenth Commandments* drive us to God's mercy.

You shall not covet your neighbor's house.

What does this mean for us?
We are to fear and love God so that we do not desire to get our neighbor's possessions by scheming, or by pretending to have a right to them, but always help him keep what is his.

You shall not covet your neighbor's wife or his manservant or his maidservant or his cattle or anything that is your neighbor's.

What does this mean for us?
We are to fear and love God so that we do not tempt or coax away from our neighbor his wife or his workers, but encourage them to remain loyal.

88

THIS IS THE CHRISTIAN FAITH: Only God Can Cleanse Man's Heart

To "covet" here means to have in one's heart a desire to have and to get something not intended for us or forbidden to us or only available at the expense of another person. Coveting is like electricity. You can't see it. You can only see what it does. A man may sit perfectly still and yet be coveting. Unless God roots out or displaces the coveting, the man will eventually *do* something evil.

Coveting begins with desiring. A man may notice that his neighbor has a fine house or car. This may lead to envy. The man becomes unhappy with his own things.

Next, he may scheme to take the neighbor's things by trickery. Perhaps he can persuade his neighbor to gamble and then cheat him.

He may *pretend to have a right* to his neighbor's goods. He may discover a way to claim his neighbor's goods legally. Sometimes a person pretends to have been badly hurt in an accident. If he brings suit and convinces the jury, the court may rule that the person who supposedly injured him must pay him a large sum of money.

He may *coax or tempt* a neighbor's wife or workers away from him. He may convince the wife that she will be happier if she leaves her husband for him. He may entice workers by offering higher wages than his neighbor can afford to pay.

89

The Bible has many examples of the results of coveting. Jezebel wanted Naboth's vineyard for her husband. She schemed to have Naboth accused of cursing the king and God. The elders and nobles obeyed her in the scheme, and so the people stoned Naboth to death. King Ahab took the vineyard.

History tells of the results of coveting. Because of it men have started wars. They have robbed and cheated and murdered. They have committed adultery.

Covetousness hints at satisfaction but produces only more greed, more sin, more unhappiness. St. Paul describes its course:

> ✠ If we have food and clothing, with these we shall be content. But those who desire to be rich fall into temptation, into a snare, into many senseless and hurtful desires that plunge men into ruin and destruction. *1 Timothy 6:8-9*

When it is left to itself, this is the way of the human heart. Men excuse themselves for it. They say: "I just want what's coming to me."

God faces men the other way. He commands that we subdue selfish desires and help our neighbor keep what is his. Instead of coaxing our neighbor's loved ones away, we are to encourage them to remain loyal.

If sins come from the heart, how can we help ourselves? Can we change what we are? We know what we *should* be like:

> You, therefore, must be perfect, as your heavenly Father is perfect. *Matthew 5:48*

Only God can change us. As we are baptized and as we hear and trust God's promises in Christ, God changes us.

> Therefore, if any one is in Christ, he is a new creation. *2 Corinthians 5:17a*

> ✠ He who abides in Me and I in him, he it is that bears much fruit, for apart from Me you can do nothing. *John 15:5*

THE CHRISTIAN BELIEVES: God's Grace Must Cleanse My Heart

In these commandments a light is flashed onto my heart. I see my true condition.

I would be foolish to try to rid my house of flies with all the windows open. So foolish would I be to try to keep from sin while my heart is not changed.

To keep any of the commandments, I must fear and love God. This is not in my heart by nature.

Alone I cannot do God's will. God's Spirit within me works to purify my heart. By Him I can love Him, obey Him, and serve my neighbor. This is my faith. By this faith I live.

Prayer Thought—

By nature I do not like to hear how wicked my heart is. I pray that God will help me to see myself honestly. I praise God for His mercy and forgiveness in Christ.

Oh, teach me, Lord, to love Thee truly
With soul and body, head and heart,
And grant me grace that I may duly
Practice fore'er love's sacred art.
Grant that my every thought may be
Directed e'er to Thee.

Hymn 399, stanza 5

16

The Conclusion of the Commandments

Our God is a jealous God.

This may seem to be a strange thing to say, yet God uses the word *jealous* to describe Himself.

A man may be jealous of his wife in the sense that because she belongs to him, he does not want her to give her love to any other man.

In a similar way God wants His people to belong to Him alone. He watches lest they give to someone else the devotion that belongs to Him alone.

God is therefore very serious about the commandments. This is seen in the *Close of the Commandments*.

> **What does God say of all these commandments?**
> He says: "I, the Lord your God, am a jealous God, visiting the iniquity of the fathers upon the children to the third and fourth generation of those who hate Me, but showing steadfast love to thousands of those who love Me and keep My commandments."

What does this mean for us?

God warns that He will punish all who break these commandments; therefore we are to fear His wrath and not disobey Him. But He promises grace and every blessing to all who keep these commandments; therefore we are to love and trust Him, and gladly do what He commands.

THIS IS THE CHRISTIAN FAITH: God's Grace Alone Can Rescue Men from Sin

We may say that God "invented" human beings. He created the first man and woman. He gave them the ability to have children. They are the original parents of the whole human race.

The manufacturer of a machine or appliance includes with his product a booklet of instructions to the user. Often one reads: "The manufacturer will not be responsible if the machine is not used properly."

The commandments are God's instructions how human beings are to live. When instructions are not followed, trouble results. God never gives up His ownership of a human being. He is not like a manufacturer who makes a product, sells it, and forgets it. God is angry and sad when any human being lives contrary to His will. He is deeply concerned.

The attempt of a human being to live contrary to God's will is *sin*. The apostle John gives a clear definition of sin:

> ✠ Everyone who commits sin is guilty of lawlessness; sin is lawlessness.
> *1 John 3:4*

Sin began when Satan rebelled against God. Created as a holy angel, he disobeyed God.

Very early in the history of the human race, Satan tempted the first parents of mankind to disobey God. Yielding to that temptation was man's first sin. One man sinned. By that act he became a sinner, and the children born to him were also sinners. Every human being since that time has been sinful by birth. Each person inherits a sinful nature. He is sinful in his origin. We say that he has original sin. St. Paul refers to this source of sinfulness:

> ✠ Sin came into the world through one man and death through sin, and so death spread to all men because all men sinned. *Romans 5:12*

Because all people are born sinners, already early in life they begin to break God's laws. They are born with a tendency to live contrary to God's will. By birth they do not fear and love God. They are enemies of God. They are not able to please God or to want to please Him. They are born guilty in God's sight. They lean toward evil.

Scriptures paint this sad picture of man without God:

> ✠ For the mind that is set on the flesh is hostile to God; it does not submit to God's law, indeed it cannot; and those who are in the flesh cannot please God. *Romans 8:7-8*

Such an infection breaks out on the surface. *Actual* sins of all kinds grow from sinful hearts. Men do what God forbids. They neglect what He commands. They think evil. They speak evil. They do evil.

God does not ignore human sin. He "visits the iniquity" of sinners upon them and their children. God punishes sin. Sometimes He acts swiftly. Sometimes He patiently delays. Sometimes other people are punished along with the sinner. The children of a drunkard may go hungry because of his sin.

Worse than any bodily penalties of sin are the spiritual costs. By his sin man loses touch with God. To break God's law is as much as to say, "I don't need you, God."

Unless something changes the picture, sin leads to eternal death. Paul is blunt about this.

✠ The wages of sin is death. *Romans 6:23a*

No man by his own ability can change the harsh facts of sin. He is born sinful. He commits sins. He makes himself an enemy of God. He is doomed to eternal death.

Our jealous God does not want men to sin. In spite of His hatred of sin He still loves and wants the sinner. God's love can do what man cannot do.

God has prepared a way by which He can punish sin and save the sinner. He gave His only Son as man's sin-bearer. Jesus bore the curse of man's sin. One who accepts Jesus as His Savior escapes God's wrath. He can be God's own child. He can live as God's child in time and in eternity.

✠ For God sent the Son into the world, not to condemn the world but that the world might be saved through Him.   *John 3:17*

THE CHRISTIAN BELIEVES: I Am a Sinner and Need a Savior

In my own life I can see sin at work. Alone, I am helpless against this dread disease. I was born with the stain of sin. I have broken God's laws. I deserve God's wrath. Only in Jesus is there hope for me. He bore also my sins. He died for me. By His grace I am released and may live for Him.

Prayer Thought—

In prayer I admit my sins and my sinfulness. I actually name my sins before God. Then I plead for forgiveness. Finally I speak my gratitude that I am a child of God for Jesus' sake.

Today Thy mercy calls us
To wash away our sin.
However great our trespass,
Whatever we have been,

However long from mercy
Our hearts have turned away,
Thy precious blood can cleanse us
And make us white today.

Hymn 279, stanza 1

95

17

Gladly Do What He Commands

Many people think God wants to take all the fun out of life.
Some decide that they don't want to miss any fun. They break the commandments and do as they please.

Others decide to try to keep the commandments. They feel that they must be miserable in this life. Then God will reward them for their misery by making them joyful in heaven.

Both classes are wrong. Sin does not lead to happiness. It only seems to. It coaxes people by offering pleasure. "If you steal, you can buy things without having to work for them," it says. Or sin says, "You will feel better if you hurt the person who hurts you." However, sin leads people to sorrow. It makes slaves of them so that they can't stop sinning even when it no longer seems to be fun.

The person who thinks that obeying God will make him miserable in this life is mistaken.

Our God is a *jealous* God. He punishes sin. Our God is also a *merciful* God. He proves this by "showing steadfast love unto thousands of those who love Him and keep His commandments." He proves it by promising "grace and every blessing to all who keep these commandments."

God wants His people to live joyfully. He makes them able to live according to His will. He frees them from the power of sin. He offers a new kind of life which begins in this world and goes on forever.

THIS IS THE CHRISTIAN FAITH: The Christian Life Is One of Glad Obedience

Christians do not try to bargain with God. They know that they cannot hope to keep His law perfectly. The commandments are strict. Human beings are born sinful. Seeing his own failure, David could only cry:

> Enter not into judgment with Thy servant, for no man living is righteous before Thee. *Psalm 143:2*

David and God's people of all ages have simply thrown themselves on God's mercy. Mercy (grace) is God's pity for people caught in their sins. God's people do not say to Him, "See how good I am!" They say, "Don't even begin to judge me. You will find too many sins."

God does not overlook sin. He is a *jealous* God. His judgment of the man who sins never changes. He says:

> The soul that sins shall die. *Ezekiel 18:4b*

Christians know a wonderful secret about God. It is a secret they share with all who will listen. God makes it possible for men to escape the curse of sin. Breaking God's law brings a curse, but –

> ✠ Christ redeemed us from the curse of the Law, having become a curse for us. *Galatians 3:13a*

What is the result if a man accepts Jesus as his Savior? There are several results. God forgives his sins. He doesn't count them against the man. The man does not have to suffer eternal punishment for them. He becomes a child of God. He will live with God forever.

He is free also to live with God in this life. He is free to serve God. He finds joy in keeping the commandments because he loves God. He is no longer afraid of God. Pleasing God is no longer a burden; it is a delight.

Trying to keep God's commandments to *earn* God's rewards makes them a heavy burden. God doesn't want the commandments to be a burden. Christians see how God has loved them in giving them a Savior. His love for them makes them love Him. A Christian is free and happy because he may keep the commandments as a loving child—not as a slave. As God's child he knows that God *gives* him what he can never *earn*. St. John's words make sense in the light of this explanation:

> ✠ For this is the love of God, that we keep His commandments. And His commandments are not burdensome. *1 John 5:3*

THE CHRISTIAN BELIEVES: I May Be Free and Joyful as a Child of God

I am God's child. I do not deserve to be. God's mercy in Christ has made me His child. As a baptized Christian, I have been adopted by God. Everything Christ has earned by His suffering and death is mine.

The sinful world tries to make me think that as a Christian I am missing good things. God assures me that the life of Christian godliness is a life of freedom and joy. I believe God when He says:

> Tell the righteous that it shall be well with them, for they shall eat the fruit of their deeds. *Isaiah 3:10*

I believe God when He tells me that "godliness is of value in every way, as it holds promise for the present life and also for the life to come." (1 Timothy 4:8)

As a child of God I have answers that others do not have. I know God made me. I know I will live with Him after death. I know that my life belongs to Him. I know that my purpose in life is to serve Him and my fellowman.

Worship is not boring. It is my privilege to speak to my God and hear Him speak to me.

I see other people as God sees them. They are sinful, yet God loves them. Jesus died for them. I am to love them even when they sin.

I have God's strength when trouble and pain come. He will never leave me. He controls trouble and pain. He is my Good Shepherd.

I trust my God. I know He loves me. He frees me from fear and selfishness and pride. Even when I fail, His love forgives me and picks me up.

God's way for me to live is the best way.

Prayer Thought—

I pray for the joy of being a Christian.
First I must ask God to forgive me when
I forget to be joyful in living for Him.
I need His protection against the devil's
lies. I ask Him to remind me of His
blessings. I ask for the gift of being
thankful.

Take, my soul, thy full salvation;
Rise o'er sin and fear and care;
Joy to find in every station,
Something still to do or bear.
Think what Spirit dwells within thee,
What a Father's smile is thine,
What a Savior died to win thee;
Child of heaven, shouldst thou repine?

Hymn 423, stanza 5

18

Law and Gospel

What does the cross mean to you? Do you think it is a pretty ornament on a necklace or your coat lapel? Do you like seeing it in your church building? The cross means so much more than this.

Someone said, "The cross is the eternal sign of how far God will go to restore a broken fellowship." The cross is a precious symbol to believing Christians, for it is the evidence of God's steadfast love for sinners. But the cross also shows God in His justice and righteousness as He condemns sin.

The whole message of the Bible is summed up in two teachings: the Law, which condemns sinners because they fail to keep God's will, and the Gospel, which tells of God's work in Christ to forgive all sin. No man can know God without these two teachings.

THIS IS THE CHRISTIAN FAITH: God Reveals Himself to Men Through Law and Gospel

Both the Law and the Gospel are the Word of God. God speaks in both. The one depends upon the other. Both Law and Gospel are to be found in the Old Testament and in the New Testament.

Every time God faces man as the righteous and almighty God, this is Law. He says:

> ✠ "You shall have no other gods before Me. . . . I the Lord your God am a jealous God."
> *Exodus 20:3-5*

Because He is God, He has the right to demand obedience from all men. Because He is just and righteous, He has the right to punish all who disobey Him. God says:

> ✠ "You shall be holy; for I the Lord your God am holy." *Leviticus 19:2*

Jesus repeats these demands of God in the words,

> ✠ "You, therefore, must be perfect, as your heavenly Father is perfect."
> *Matthew 5:48*

Every human being knows something about God's law. He knows something about power and authority. He knows something about punishment for wrong. Every human being has a conscience. Conscience is the individual's sense of right and wrong. It needs the instruction of God's Word. St. Paul writes:

> When Gentiles, who have not the Law, do by nature what the Law requires, they are a law unto themselves, even though they do not have the Law. They show that what the Law requires is written on their hearts, while their conscience also bears witness and their conflicting thoughts accuse or perhaps excuse them.
> *Romans 2:14-15*

The Law shows man his helplessness before God's demands for righteousness. It condemns and kills men in that it shows men their unrighteousness. It draws the line of separation between the holy God and sinful man.

The Gospel is the Word of God which supersedes the Law. It is God's last and most important Word. The Gospel is the good news that God in Christ Jesus reaches down to sinful man. God in Christ meets all the claims and demands of the Law in man's place. The Gospel proclaims the fact that God in Jesus Christ crosses the line of separation between Himself and sinful man.

101

God gave His only-begotten Son to the world to accomplish this great deed. Jesus is God's living Word. St. Paul describes this in the words,

> ✠ God was in Christ reconciling the world to Himself, not counting their trespasses against them. . . . For our sake He made Him to be sin who knew no sin, so that in Him we might become the righteousness of God. *2 Corinthians 5:19-21*

No man is born with the Gospel inside him, as he has the Law written in his heart. Someone has to proclaim this news to him. God started the Gospel in the garden of Eden. The Gospel is God working in Jesus Christ to reconcile sinners. The Gospel is God working in the Holy Spirit. God is at work when we tell this Gospel to each other.

The Gospel is not only God's invitation to forgiveness, it is also the power of God which draws sinners to Himself. The Gospel is in Holy Baptism, in which God makes a sinner His own child.

THE CHRISTIAN BELIEVES: God Reveals Himself to Me in Law and Gospel

God judges me every day. Daily I am faced with my weakness and sin. Every day finds me thinking that I can get even with God by doing something good by myself. I am ashamed how often I love myself or something else more than God.

God's mercies are new to me daily. God is faithful to His promises. His Word is sure. In the life, death, and resurrection of Jesus God forgives me all my sins. He makes me a new person when His Holy Spirit lives in me. Now I can do works which please Him. He gives me that power.

In my baptism God made me His child. Every day I confess my sin to Him. Every day He forgives me. Every day He gives me power to live for Him.

Prayer Thought—

I confess my sin to God. I thank God
for His everlasting love and mercy to me.
I thank Him for making me His child.
I pray for His Spirit in my life to make me
also a good ambassador of His Gospel.

The Gospel shows the Father's grace,
Who sent His Son to save our race,
Proclaims how Jesus lived and died
That man might thus be justified.

May we in faith its tidings learn
Nor thanklessly its blessings spurn;
May we in faith its truth confess
And praise the Lord our Righteousness!

Hymn 297, stanzas 1 and 6

19

Proclaiming Law and Gospel

The revelation of God contains two main doctrines: the Law and the Gospel. Both are the Word of God. But we must keep these doctrines separate from each other; they must not be mixed.

A chemist can tell us how two helpful substances are turned into poison when they are mixed. This is what could happen when Law and Gospel are mixed.

Dr. C. F. W. Walther, first president of The Lutheran Church—Missouri Synod, illustrated this by colors. When you mix yellow with blue, it is no longer yellow or blue but green. When we mix Law and Gospel, we get a third thing that is neither Law nor Gospel.

We can understand a clear definition of Law and a clear definition of Gospel. But to put Law and Gospel into practice in life is difficult. Only God's Holy Spirit can teach us how to keep Law and Gospel separate as we proclaim them both.

THIS IS THE CHRISTIAN FAITH: Each Christian Must Proclaim the Law and the Gospel Correctly

In the process of becoming followers of God, sinners need the Law. To be a Christian means to trust in Jesus as Savior. That sounds very simple. Because all men are sinful, it is not simple at all.

Two things keep men from accepting Jesus as their Savior. First, they may not admit that anything needs to be done to make them acceptable to God. Second, if anything needs to be done, they feel that they can do it themselves. They do not understand that only a perfect life satisfies God. The Gospel is not for people who do not yet feel their sin. They will not rejoice at having a Savior.

The Law brands all men as sinners. It reveals God's anger at sin.

> ✠ For the wrath of God is revealed from heaven against all ungodliness and wickedness of men.   *Romans 1:18a*

The Law must make them aware of their need. This it does very clearly.

> ✠ None is righteous, no, not one; no one understands, no one seeks for God. All have turned aside; together they have gone wrong; no one does good, not even one.   *Romans 3:10-12*

Only the sinner who feels the lash of the Law is ready for the Gospel. Martin Luther compared a sinner's heart to a field. It must first be plowed by the Law. Then the seed of the Gospel will have a place in which to grow.

To become followers of God, sinners need the Gospel. A man may see his sin and be frightened. He is not a Christian until he also turns to Jesus as His only Savior. As he hears the Gospel, the Holy Spirit invites him to believe. The Holy Spirit makes it possible for him to believe promises like this one:

> ✠ I, I am He who blots out your transgressions for My own sake, and I will not remember your sins.   *Isaiah 43:25*

Both Law and Gospel work to make followers of God. The Law does not make believers. It only strikes hard to drive people to feel their own helplessness, and in the Gospel they turn to Jesus Christ as their only Savior.

Even after a person is a believer he needs the Law and Gospel.

105

A believer still sins. Sin keeps edging into his life. He is tempted on every side.

Every day the Christian needs the Law. His sinful nature needs to be shown up every day. Otherwise he begins again to trust his own goodness. He needs to be driven back to Christ again and again.

Every day the Christian needs the Gospel. The good news of God's love and forgiveness is a comfort to him. Many forces pick at the Christian. They try to make him doubt God's love. Every day the repentant Christian needs to be reassured that –

> ✠ He Himself bore our sins in His body on the tree, that we might die to sin and live to righteousness. By His wounds you have been healed.
> *1 Peter 2:24*

THE CHRISTIAN BELIEVES: I Need Law and Gospel Daily in My Life

In the Law God shows me my sins. He condemns me for trying to take pride in what I can do. I can never find salvation in the Law. The Law shows me how helpless I am before God. I need this message every day.

In the Gospel God invites me to be His child. He shows me all that He has done in Jesus Christ to forgive me all my sins. He draws me to Him in this very invitation. I need this message every day.

I know that only God's Holy Spirit can teach me how to keep Law and Gospel separate. I need to know that a proud sinner must hear the Law. But a repentant sinner needs the Gospel.

Prayer Thought—

> I confess all my sins, especially the sins
> of pride. I ask for the enlightenment of
> the Holy Spirit so that I may proclaim
> Law and Gospel rightly. I praise God for
> His salvation.

> My guilt, O Father, Thou hast laid
> On Christ, Thy Son, my Savior.
> Lord Jesus, Thou my debt hast paid
> And gained for me God's favor.
> O Holy Ghost, Thou Fount of grace,
> The good in me to Thee I trace;
> In faith do Thou preserve me.
>
> *Hymn 375, stanza 5*

"We too believe, and so we speak"
2 Corinthians 4:13

Section III: The Apostles' Creed

20. The Creeds of the Church
21. God, the Maker of All
22. God, the Provider and Protector
23. Thank God for His Goodness
24. Our Lord Jesus Christ
25. Jesus Is God and Man
26. Jesus, Our Redeemer
27. Prophet, Priest, and King
28. That I May Be His Own
29. The Holy Spirit
30. The Holy Spirit at Work in Me
31. The Holy Christian Church
32. Where Is the Church?
33. The Broken Church
34. The Church in Action
35. The Resurrection of the Body
36. Eternal Life

20

The Creeds of the Church

What makes a person a Christian?

The way he looks on the outside has nothing to do with it. A Christian may be young or old. Some Christians are rich; others are poor. Christians are found in many nations and among all races.

Moreover, we can't always tell a Christian by his speech and actions. Christians are not perfect. They admit that they still sin. We see, too, that many non-Christians are gentle and kind.

God makes a person a Christian by calling him to faith. This faith will change the way he lives. It is his faith that makes him a Christian.

A Christian person, then, believes what God tells him in the Bible about what He has done for him. It is not enough just to *know* about what God has done for mankind. A Christian accepts God's promises as true. By faith he relies on what God has done for him through Jesus.

A Christian does not believe merely that there is a God. He believes that God is *his* God.

Such faith is invisible. No man can see it. Only God and the person himself can know whether a person believes. Moreover, Christians believe things that can't be seen. That is what faith is — trust in things which are not seen. The Bible explains faith that way:

> Now faith is the assurance of things hoped for, the conviction of things not seen.
> *Hebrews 11:1*

Christians have never been content just to believe for themselves. They try to get others to believe the good news about Jesus. To do this, they learn to tell about their faith. They find that they can put their faith into words. Jesus commanded believers to share their faith. He said:

> So everyone who acknowledges Me before men, I also will acknowledge before My Father who is in heaven.
> *Matthew 10:32*

Later, God's people began to write their faith in words. A man would write a letter to tell what he believed about God. Someone else would read it. Together they would say, "This letter says what we both believe."

The Latin word for "I believe" is *credo*. When a man wrote what he believed about God, he called it his "I believe." In Latin he called it his *credo*. From that Latin word we get our word "creed." A creed is a statement of what people believe.

There have been many written statements of the Christian faith. Some were long, some short. Some have been lost, some passed down through the ages. Any Christian may write a creed. That is, he may write what he believes about his God. Sometimes groups of God's people meet to talk about their faith. Together they write a statement of what they believe according to what they have drawn from God's Word.

Among all the creeds that have been written, three are outstanding. Nearly all Christians know and use them. We call them the three general creeds of the church. They state in beautiful words what Christians believe.

One is called the Apostles' Creed. It had its beginning in the time of the early church. It is a summary of what the apostles wrote in the Bible.

Another creed is the Nicene Creed. It is named after the city of Nicaea, where the first statement of this creed was written and accepted by a church council. Some men had begun to teach false ideas about God and especially about Jesus Christ. Leaders of the church met to discuss the problem; they agreed on this clear statement of what Christians believe.

111

The third general creed is the Athanasian Creed. It is named after a great Christian teacher, Athanasius. It too sets forth Bible truth in the face of false teachings regarding the Trinity.

None of these creeds is in the Bible in so many words. Each of them sums up the teachings of the Bible. By speaking these creeds we join millions of Christians in confessing our faith. We are even able to use the very same words that Christians of previous ages have used.

The creeds are not just to be spoken. That is a mistake some people make. We are to confess the creeds. That is, we make the words our own. When we say the creeds we mean, "This the church believes. I believe it, too."

God's Holy Spirit enables us to *believe* what the creeds say. They tell us that God made all things. They speak of His love in sending Jesus as our Savior. They tell of the work of the Holy Spirit for us.

God is at work in us, enabling us to live in a manner that shows that He is our God. We can trust Jesus.

We can share our faith with others. This is called witnessing. The creeds help us by giving us the words to use when we witness.

We will need to study the creeds. The creeds are an outline that helps us understand the Bible.

We say the creeds. We confess the creeds. We live in the light of the creeds. We are part of God's confessing people. The long parade of Christians marches through the centuries. The parade is on the way to heaven. By God's grace we are part of it.

Prayer Thought—

I can *say* the creeds by my own ability.
To believe what they say and to live by
them, I need God's grace. Therefore I pray
for the Holy Spirit's work in me. As I
study the creeds, I ask God to strengthen
my faith in Him and what He does for me.

Through the night of doubt and sorrow
Onward goes the pilgrim band,
Singing songs of expectation,
Marching to the Promised Land.
Clear before us, through the darkness,
Gleams and burns the guiding light.
Brother clasps the hand of brother,
Stepping fearless through the night.

One the strain the lips of thousands
Lift as from the heart of one;
One the conflict, one the peril,
One the march in God begun;
One the gladness of rejoicing
On the far eternal shore,
Where the one almighty Father
Reigns in love forevermore.

Hymn 481, stanzas 1 and 3

21

God, the Maker of All

Where did the world and everything in it come from? That is one of the oldest of all the questions people ask. Scientists and other thinkers are still searching for the answer. The very first sentence of the Bible is the answer God's people accept in faith. It says:

In the beginning God created the heavens and the earth.

Genesis 1:1

Christians begin the Apostles' Creed by stating in the *First Article* their faith in God as the Maker of all things.

CREATION

**I believe in God the Father Almighty,
Maker of heaven and earth.**

What does this mean?

I believe that God has created me and all that exists. He has given me and still preserves my body and soul with all their powers.

THIS IS THE CHRISTIAN FAITH: God Made All People and Things

When Christians confess their faith, they say, "I believe." They could say, "We believe," since this faith is held by millions of people. But each person must believe for himself. He cannot believe for another person, and nobody else can believe for him. Each Christian must feel attached to God as David felt when he wrote:

> But I trust in Thee, O Lord; I say, "Thou art my God." *Psalm 31:14*

When Christians say they *believe* in God, they mean that they believe God is. However, that is only a small part of what it means to believe in God. To believe in God means to trust Him. It means to depend upon Him. No one wholly understands God. What He says in the Bible and what He does leads Christians to rely on His promises.

When Christians confess that God is their *Father,* they are telling what God means to them. A child gets his life from his father. A good earthly father cares about his children. He provides food, clothing, and shelter. He calls a physician when they are ill. He corrects them. He teaches and guides them. In many ways he shows his love for them.

God is a Father to believers in a much greater way. Sometimes God is called the Father of all people because He made all people. People of all races trace themselves back to a single creative act of God. In a very special way God is the Father of those who accept Jesus as their Savior. Jesus kept the Law for all people. To those who believe that, He gives the right to be the children of God. In God's sight it makes no difference what color skin a man may have or what country he lives in. God wants all people to be His sons and heirs.

> For in Christ Jesus you are all sons of God, through faith.
>
> *Galatians 3:26*

When Christians call God *almighty, the Maker of heaven and earth,* they express their faith in one of God's great acts. With great wisdom and power God made everything that exists. The first two chapters of the Bible tell about God calling the world into being. God's people have always had an answer to the question, "Where did the world come from?" They reply, "We believe that God made it." The apostle says it this way:

> ✠ By faith we understand that the world was created by the Word of God, so that what is seen was made out of things which do not appear.
>
> *Hebrews 11:3*

115

God made everything good. We can see His wisdom and goodness when we study God's world. A budding flower, the pattern of a spider's web, a graceful fawn, and many other objects and animals show the wonder of God's world. Science is the study of how God made the world and how man can use all that God made.

As the crown of His creation, God made *human beings*. He made them perfect and without sin. In that way they were like God. That is why the Bible tells of the creation of human beings in these words:

> ✠ So God created man in His own image, in the image of God He created him; male and female He created them.   *Genesis 1:27*

Human beings are not advanced animals. They are special creatures. God made man and directed him to control the universe. Man discovers the riches of God's wisdom. He is to use them in such a way that they reflect God's love. Besides this, human beings are made to live with God forever. People have lost this privilege by rebelling against God. God sent His Son to restore that privilege by His sacrifice.

THE CHRISTIAN BELIEVES: God Made and Cares for My Body and Soul

I believe that I am God's child. He made me. Through my parents He gave me my body and my soul. Every day He gives me all that I need for my body. Sometimes He uses my parents and other people to give me what I need. He is the Savior of my body and soul. This is my faith.

How will this faith show in my life? It will show when what I do reveals the work of God's Spirit in me. He enables me to worship, to trust my God especially in days of trouble, to respect and care for the body He has given me, and to treat other people with respect because God made them too. Without confessing my faith in words, I reveal to other people that I believe by the way I live.

✠ The spirit of God has made me, and the breath of the Almighty gives me life.

Job 33:4

Prayer Thought—

> Each person receives various blessings
> from God. As I think of God as my Maker,
> I will first want to list some of the things
> He has given me. I will take special note
> of my body and soul and all their powers.
> I will not forget the blessings that come
> to me through Jesus, my Savior. For each
> blessing I will praise and thank Him.

Praise to the Lord, the Almighty, the King of creation!
O my soul, praise Him, for He is thy Health and Salvation!
Join the full throng; Wake, harp and psalter and song;
Sound forth in glad adoration!

Praise to the Lord, who hath fearfully, wondrously made thee;
Health hath vouchsafed and, when heedlessly falling, hath stayed thee.
What need or grief ever hath failed of relief?—
Wings of His mercy did shade thee.

Hymn 39, stanzas 1 and 3

117

22

God the Provider and Protector

The world cannot get more than two seconds away from God.
By that we mean that all people and the whole world depend upon God for life. What would happen if God stopped doing the things He alone can do? Disaster would follow. Men would die, and the world would be destroyed.

Not all people think that God provides for the world. Many just take the sun and rain and seeds for granted. They give themselves credit for what they have.

Christians look to God to provide for them, protect them, and guide them. We express our faith in God as Provider and Protector when we say in the *First Article:*

> He provides me with food and clothing, home and family, daily work, and all I need from day to day. God also protects me in time of danger and guards me from every evil.

THIS IS THE CHRISTIAN FAITH: God Provides for and Protects His People

God's people believe that He is responsible for the way the world produces food. God's wisdom placed the sun at just the proper distance from the earth. By His will the planets move in their orbits. The winds blow according to His plan. They carry clouds filled with water for fields and forests.

Who teaches bees to gather nectar and make honey? Why are there so many different kinds of vegetables? These and hundreds of other questions the Christians answer by saying, "We believe God arranges it all." Long ago God showed His control of the world when He promised:

> While the earth remains, seedtime and harvest, cold and heat, summer and winter, day and night shall not cease.   *Genesis 8:22*

God does not give us the things we need unless we work. Men work as farmers or factory workers. Together, they are able to get from the earth the things they need. God provides daily work and its reward.

God gives homes and families to provide love and care for us. A snug kitchen, a clean bed, a mother to care for the family, a father to pay the bills among other things—these are God's gifts.

In thankfulness God's people confess with David:

> The eyes of all look to Thee, and Thou givest them their food in due season. Thou openest Thy hand, Thou satisfiest the desire of every living thing.   *Psalm 145:15-16*

Yes, even to unbelievers and the unthankful, God is the Provider.

God protects from danger and harm. He often uses human means to accomplish this. He gives men wisdom and common sense to meet

119

danger and defend themselves. He works through the officials of good government to protect and defend people.

God uses also His holy angels to protect His people. Angels are spirits, very strong and countless in number. The psalmist said it in the words:

> ✠ The angel of the Lord encamps around those who fear Him and delivers them. *Psalm 34:7*

Yet believers may suffer from an accident. They get sick. They face trouble and pain. Christians, too, may be crippled or blind. Sin's consequences touch the lives of all people, including those of God's people.

God uses these experiences to make His people stronger in their faith. God teaches us to trust Him for everything when He lets trouble enter our lives. God showed His steadfast love when He gave His Son as our Savior. Even in heartache and death we can count on God's love and concern because of Jesus. The prophet gives us this comforting promise of God:

> Fear not, for I have redeemed you; I have called you by name, you are Mine. When you pass through the waters, I will be with you; and through the rivers, they shall not overwhelm you. *Isaiah 43:1-2a*

THE CHRISTIAN BELIEVES: My Life Is in God's Powerful, Loving Hands

I trust God to take care of me when I die. I trust Him to take care of me while I am living.

God provides just what I need. I need not worry, for that would show lack of trust. I should not be greedy. I am not to be so eager to get His good gifts for myself that I forget to share them with others.

Pain and trouble may come to me. Even then God will be protecting me. He has promised never to forsake me. His angels surround me. He is in control of my life. What happens to me happens by His will.

I am free to work hard at the tasks He sends. My God even helps me hold to my faith in Him. The Holy Spirit strengthens me by God's Word. Believing all this, I may honestly join the chorus of God's people as they confess:

> ✠ Great is the Lord and greatly to be praised, and His greatness is unsearchable. *Psalm 145:3*

I will *confess* the times I have failed to
trust God. I will *thank* Him for His care
for me. I will *ask* for His continued
guidance.

O God of Jacob, by whose hand
Thy people still are fed;
Who through this weary pilgrimage
Hast all our fathers led.

Through each perplexing path of life
Our wandering footsteps guide;
Give us each day our daily bread
And raiment fit provide.

Oh, spread Thy covering wings around
Till all our wanderings cease
And at our Father's loved abode
Our souls arrive in peace.

Hymn 434, stanzas 1, 3, and 4

121

23

Thank God for His Goodness

People who do not believe in God do not know who should get the credit for good things that happen to them.

Sometimes they give themselves the credit. However, they become uneasy about this. Therefore they may simply speak of the "good luck" that comes their way.

The child of God knows the source of his blessings. He believes that he has an all-powerful and loving Father who blesses him. And the Christian believes that he is to show in his life how he feels about his generous God.

This is beautifully expressed in the last words of the explanation of the *First Article* of the Apostles' Creed.

> All this He does out of fatherly and divine goodness and mercy, though I do not deserve it. Therefore I surely ought to thank and praise, serve and obey Him. This is most certainly true.

THIS IS THE CHRISTIAN FAITH: Christians Thank God for Goodness Which They Do Not Deserve

God is not good to people because they deserve it. No one can bargain with God. A man who works for another man gets a paycheck at the end of the week. He deserves it. He has earned it. He has a right to it.

No human being has a right to anything from God. All people fail to live up to what God expects. If we begin to speak about what we deserve from God, we will soon be speaking about punishment. Anyone who knows God's law and how far all people fall short of keeping it, does not want God to give him what he *deserves.* He urges God not to give him what he deserves, saying:

> If Thou, O Lord, shouldst mark iniquities, Lord, who could stand?
>
> *Psalm 130:3*

Not our deserving but God's "fatherly, divine goodness and mercy" cause Him to bless men.

Christians believe that God's goodness moves Him to be good to men. God *is* good. Because He is God, He delights in blessing His creatures. St. John says, "God is love." (1 John 4:8b)

Christians believe that God's mercy moves Him to be good to men. Mercy is undeserved kindness. In the story of the prodigal son the father forgave his son and welcomed him back with gifts. He deserved to be scolded and punished. That story tells us what God is like.

Many of God's people have tried to describe the greatness of God's mercy. The prophet Jeremiah wrote:

> ✠ The steadfast love of the Lord never ceases, His mercies never come to an end; they are new every morning; great is Thy faithfulness.
>
> *Lamentations 3:22-23*

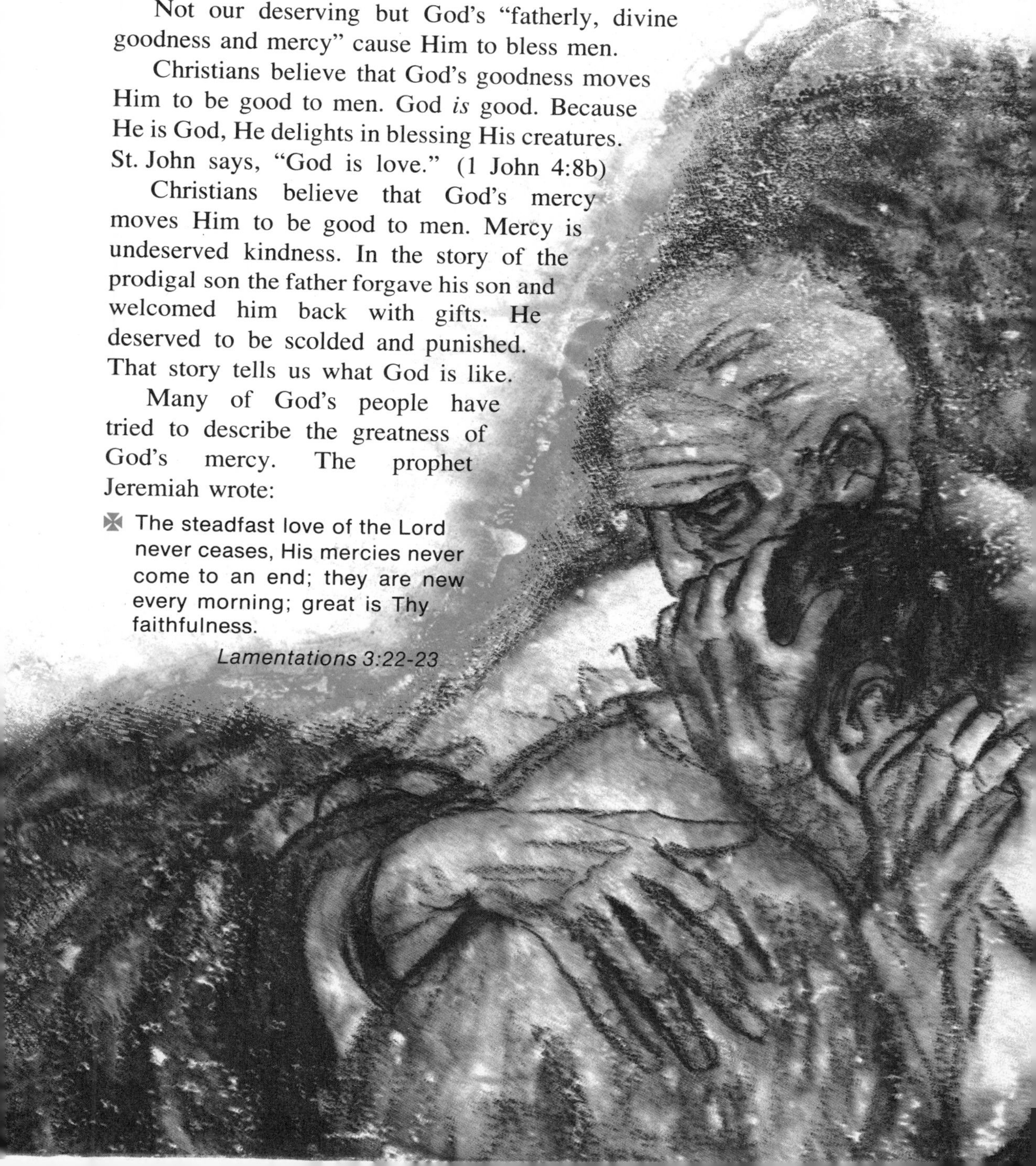

Such goodness and mercy we call "divine" because only God can be so kind and patient. We call God's goodness "fatherly" because only He who loves as a good father can care so much for children who do not deserve it.

God's people can hardly find words to express their wonder at a God who loves so freely and gives so much. They look for other ways of praising Him. Much of the world's great music and painting and building gives expression to the praise of God's people. Many have written poems and hymns. Others have painted pictures or built cathedrals. Composers have written great music, and choirs have praised Him in great hymns. All have tried to find ways to say with the psalmist:

> O give thanks to the Lord, for He is good; His steadfast love endures forever! *Psalm 118:1*

But God's people do not always dedicate their lives to God. They fall into the temptations of the devil. All sinners want to take pride in their good works and achievements. They even think they can repay God for His goodness by their noble deeds.

God forgives also this sin of pride. Remembering our baptism, we drown our feelings of selfishness. God's Spirit makes us new people. We are His people, with the ability to praise Him in words and deeds. We can make Joshua's promise a motto for our lives too:

> ✠ As for me and my house, we will serve the Lord. *Joshua 24:15b*

THE CHRISTIAN BELIEVES: My Life Is to Show My Thankfulness to My God

My life is a story of how God is good to His child. He gives me all I need for my body and my soul. I too have sinned. I have no right to expect His goodness.

But He forgives me my pride, selfishness, and ingratitude. By His Spirit He enables me to worship Him. Yes, my whole life is my praise to Him. Every new day I want to remember that God works in me to show His glory.

Prayer Thought—

I may begin my prayer meditation by
reading Psalm 100. Then I may pray
specifically that God will show me ways
in which I may serve Him in my daily
life. If I have been thoughtless and
thankless, I will want to confess that
and ask for forgiveness.

O Lord of heaven and earth and sea,
To Thee all praise and glory be.
How shall we show our love to Thee, Who givest all?

Thou didst not spare Thine only Son,
But gav'st Him for a world undone,
And freely with that Blessed One Thou givest all.

For souls redeemed, for sins forgiven,
For means of grace and hopes of heaven,
What can to Thee, O Lord, be given, Who givest all?

Hymn 443, stanzas 1, 4, and 6

24

Our Lord Jesus Christ

A Christian is a person who believes that Jesus Christ is his Lord and Savior.

To understand why Christians believe this, it is necessary to know who Jesus is and what He has done.

Christians have written thousands of books about Jesus. But all we need to know about Him is in the Bible. The first four books of the New Testament explain His life and work for sinners. First it is helpful to know the whole story of Jesus in brief form.

THIS IS THE CHRISTIAN FAITH: **Jesus Is God's Son, Who Came to Save All Men**

The Son of God never had a beginning. He was always God. He existed before the world was made.

He was in the beginning with God. *John 1:2*

God decided to enter into the world as a human being. To bring this about, God chose a young woman named Mary to be the mother and sent an angel to tell the Virgin Mary that the baby would be God's Son. She and Joseph were to take care of the baby. They called Him Jesus, a name that means "Savior." In this way God's Son received His human body and became a human being. Of this divine baby the angel said:

For to you is born this day in the city of David a Savior, who is Christ the Lord.
Luke 2:11

Jesus was born in Bethlehem, a small city in Palestine. He was raised by Mary and Joseph in the town of Nazareth. He is sometimes called Jesus of Nazareth. As a boy He helped His earthly father in his work as a carpenter. Sometimes Jesus is called the Carpenter of Nazareth. He never stopped being God. He laid aside God's power to become lowly and humble. At times He used this power to show He was God's Son.

For about 30 years Jesus lived a quiet life. Then He began what we call His public ministry. He began to do the work for which He had become a human being.

First He chose 12 men from His disciples to be His special helpers. We call them apostles. After Jesus had finished His work, they went out to spread the good news of the Savior around the world.

For nearly 3 years Jesus visited the cities and villages of His country. At first people thought He was just another traveling teacher. However, His words and actions soon made people flock to hear Him.

He said He was the Son of God. He said He had come from heaven. He said He was the world's Savior. He said people could live forever if they believed in Him.

127

He performed many miracles. He did things that only God can do. He changed water into wine; He walked on the sea; He healed people who were ill; He made deaf men hear. He caused the blind to see. Hopeless cripples walked when He touched them. He even brought dead people back to life.

The leaders of His own religion and country became jealous of Him. He knew that many of them were evil, dishonest men. He told them so. In return they plotted to kill Him.

After Jesus had been teaching for about 3 years, they arrested Him. They found Him guilty of saying He was God's Son. The Roman governor ordered His execution. Soldiers nailed Him to a cross. Jesus died, and His friends buried Him.

Jesus did not stay dead. He was killed on a Friday. On Sunday morning He appeared alive again. Many people saw and touched Him. During 40 days He showed Himself alive to His disciples. Then He went back to heaven. From a hilltop He rose miraculously into the sky until a cloud hid Him.

The story does not end there. Jesus' followers believe that He is with them even though they cannot see Him. They also believe that He will come to earth again to judge all men. Angels told His friends that He will return:

> ✠ This Jesus, who was taken up from you into heaven, will come in the same way as you saw Him go into heaven. *Acts 1:11b*

Christians confess that Jesus came, taught, suffered, died, and rose again. He came to rescue men from the power of evil and to make it possible for them to live as God's own people in this world and forever. He will come again on the Last Day to judge the world.

THE CHRISTIAN BELIEVES: Jesus Is My Lord and Savior

Jesus did His work for all men. It all happened hundreds of years ago. Yet He came and lived and died and rose again for *me*.

I want to be saved. I want my sins forgiven. I want to live as God's child. I want to live forever. I know that my only hope for all this is found in Jesus.

The story of God's great act in sending Jesus is important to me. My mind and heart are eager to know and understand more about it.

The story of Jesus' life fills me with
wonder. God stooped so low to save me.
My prayer will praise His goodness.
I will also pray for a strong faith in my
Lord and Savior.

All praise to Thee, eternal God,
Who, clothed in garb of flesh and blood,
Dost take a manger for Thy throne,
While worlds on worlds are Thine alone.
Hallelujah!

All this for us Thy love hath done;
By this to Thee our love is won;
For this our joyful songs we raise
And shout our thanks in ceaseless praise.
Hallelujah!

Hymn 80, stanzas 1 and 6

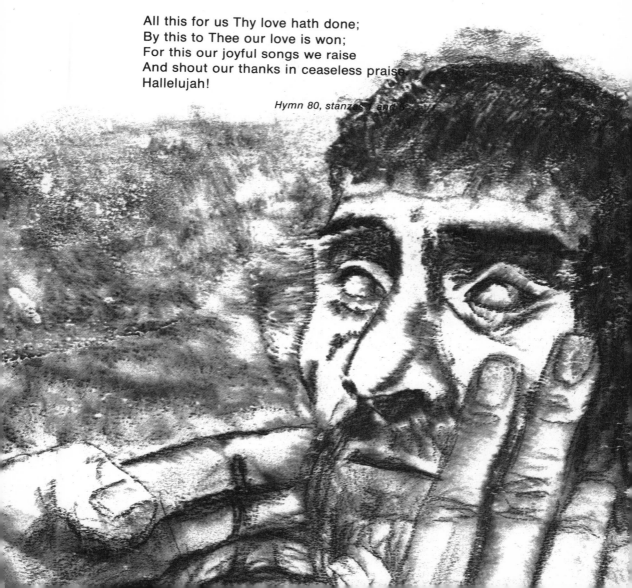

25

Jesus Is God and Man

Pointing to Jesus, the high priest shouted, "What is your judgment?"

Jesus stood before the chief judges of His nation on the night before He was crucified. Because they were proud and jealous, they answered, "He deserves death." That was *their* judgment.

The followers of Jesus have given a much different answer. They give their opinion of Jesus in the words of the *Second Article* of the Apostles' Creed.

And in Jesus Christ, His only Son, our Lord, who was conceived by the Holy Ghost, born of the Virgin Mary, suffered under Pontius Pilate, was crucified, dead, and buried; He descended into hell; the third day He rose again from the dead; He ascended into heaven and sitteth on the right hand of God the Father Almighty, from thence He shall come to judge the quick and the dead.

What does this mean?

I believe that Jesus Christ—true God, Son of the Father from eternity, and true man, born of the Virgin Mary—is my Lord.

THIS IS THE CHRISTIAN FAITH: Jesus Is God and Man, Savior and Lord

Christians believe that Jesus is God. They believe that He is also a human being. That is why they call Him the God-man.

In many places and in many ways the Bbile pictures Jesus as GOD.

God the Father, angels, and apostles called Him by *God's names.* When He was born, angels said He was "a Savior, who is Christ the Lord" (Luke 2:11). Peter confessed: "You are the Christ, the Son of the living

God" (Matthew 16:16). Thomas called Him "My Lord and my God" (John 20:28). God the Father called Him "My beloved Son." (Matthew 3:17)

When the Bible writers *describe* Jesus, they say things about Him which can be said only about God. He has no beginning—"He was in the beginning with God" (John 1:2). He made all things—"All things were made through Him" (John 1:3). He is everywhere at once—"I am with you always" (Matthew 28:20b). He does not change—"Jesus Christ is the same yesterday and today and for ever" (Hebrews 13:8). He has God's power and glory—"For in Him the whole fullness of deity dwells bodily." (Colossians 2:9)

Before many eyewitnesses Jesus *did* things that only God can do. He forgave sins—"The Son of man has authority on earth to forgive sins" (Matthew 9:6). He healed the sick. He brought dead people back to life. He walked on the sea. He came back to life after He had been killed.

The early followers of Jesus accepted Him as God. His followers of all ages confess that He is God. Therefore, they *worship* Jesus. He is their Lord. He is Lord of all people, whether they accept Him or not.

The same Scriptures that tell us Jesus is God also tell us that He is man. Jesus had no earthly father. Yet He was born as a human child, and

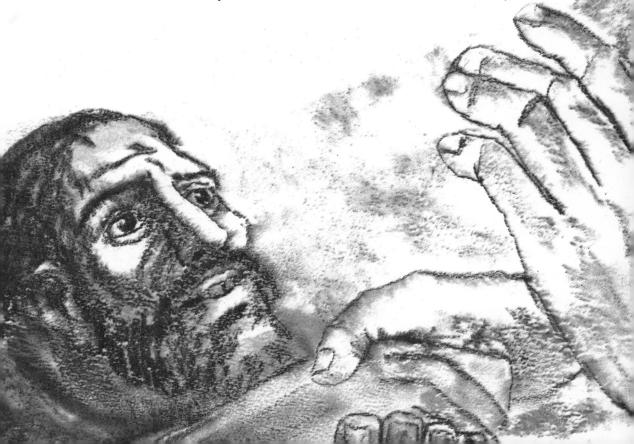

the Virgin Mary was His earthly mother. He had a human body. He ate and drank and slept and walked and talked. When nails pierced His hands, He bled. Even after He rose from the grave, He was still human. He said:

> ✠ See My hands and My feet, that it is I Myself; handle Me and see; for a spirit has not flesh and bones as you see that I have. *Luke 24:39*

Christians believe that Jesus is the Redeemer of whom the Old Testament speaks. He is the Christ. "Christ" means the "Anointed One." Kings and priests were anointed with oil when they began their work. Jesus was chosen and set apart by God the Father for the work of saving all people. No other person could do it. Only the God-man could be the Savior.

Jesus Christ, true God, became also a true man. He became "incarnate." That means He took a human body.

The penalty for sin is suffering and death. Jesus had to be human to be able to suffer and die. But not just anyone's suffering and death would do. Only the suffering and death of the perfect Son of God could atone for all sins of all people. Jesus is the only possible Savior, for He alone is God *and* man.

> ✠ It was fitting that we should have such a high priest, holy, blameless, unstained, separated from sinners, exalted above the heavens. *Hebrews 7:26*

God's holy Son did not hesitate to give His life to redeem mankind.

> ✠ You know that you were ransomed . . . not with perishable things such as silver or gold, but with the precious blood of Christ, like that of a lamb without blemish or spot. *1 Peter 1:18-19*

THE CHRISTIAN BELIEVES: Jesus Is My Lord and God, My Savior

By my baptism I became a member of the church and a child of God. The church's confession is my confession.

Jesus is my God. His power and love save me from my sins. He is able to help me in every trouble. He hears and answers my prayers. I worship Him as my God.

I am glad that Jesus became also a human being. He understands me. As a human being He could die for my sins and break the power of death.

God is not distant and strange to me. The Son of God became a baby, a child, a youth, a human being.

I cannot understand how Jesus can be both God and man. I am only glad that my God fulfills my needs so well.

I pray for faith to accept Jesus as my
God and Lord. I wonder at the sacrifice
He made in becoming human to save me.
I thank Him for His great kindness.

Christ, by highest heaven adored,
Christ, the everlasting Lord,
Late in time behold Him come,
Offspring of a virgin's womb.
Veiled in flesh the Godhead see,
Hail th' incarnate Deity!
Pleased as Man with man to dwell;
Jesus, our Immanuel!
Hark! the herald angels sing,
"Glory to the newborn King!"

Hymn 94, stanza 2

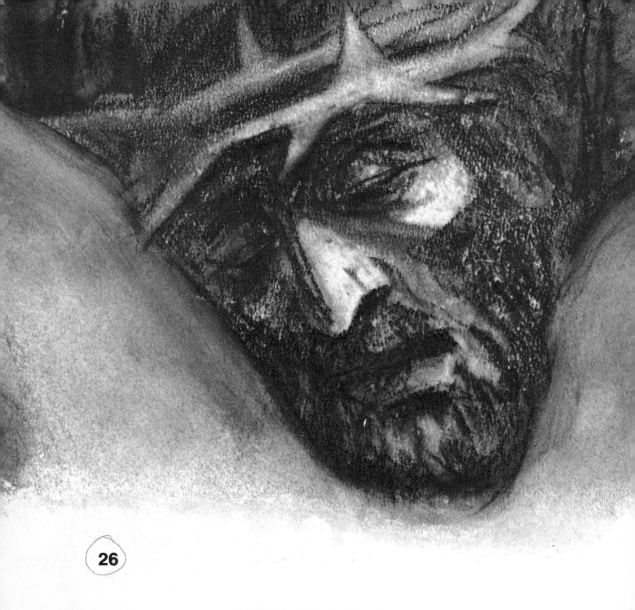

26

Jesus, Our Redeemer

Christians worship Jesus as their God. They worship Him for what He *is*.

They also worship Him for what He *has done* for them and for all people.

In explaining the *Second Article* of the Apostles' Creed, Luther included a clear statement about Jesus' work for us. It is Jesus—

At great cost He has saved and redeemed me, a lost and condemned person. He has freed me from sin, death, and the power of the devil —not with silver or gold, but with His holy and precious blood and His innocent suffering and death.

THIS IS THE CHRISTIAN FAITH: Jesus Suffered and Died to Save All Men

Jesus carried our guilt to get us out of trouble. No one can appreciate being saved by Jesus until he admits his deep trouble as a sinner. He must first see himself as a "lost and condemned" person.

Without Jesus all people are lost. They are lost from God and will be lost from heaven. Scripture says:

Your iniquities have made a separation between you and your God.
Isaiah 59:2a

Without Jesus all people are condemned. They must bear full blame for all their sins. Scripture says that anyone who breaks God's law is under a curse.

Cursed be he who does not confirm the words of this law by doing them. *Deuteronomy 27:26a*

Jesus has redeemed and saved us from this curse. In our place He did His Father's will perfectly. In our place He bore the curse we deserve. Jesus left no doubt why He became a man. He said:

The Son of Man came to seek and to save the lost. *Luke 19:10*

The trouble from which Jesus redeemed us has three names: sin, death, and the power of the devil. These are the "unholy three."

A man *sins* when he disobeys God's law. He may seem to get away with it. However, whenever he sins he adds to his guilt. He builds up more of God's anger against him. Worse yet, sin has a power to make people want to keep on sinning. It makes slaves of people by forcing them to sin even after they want to stop. God's answer for the terrible power of sin is to tell us:

. . . He [Jesus] is the expiation for our sins, and . . . for the sins of the whole world. *1 John 2:2*

Death is another foe that has been conquered by Christ. Since Christ broke the power of eternal death, death for the Christian is really only the door to eternal life. Although the body must still die, even as Christ died and rose again, we too will rise with glorified bodies and enjoy eternal life with Him.

St. Paul says:

> ✠ Christ Jesus . . . abolished death and brought life and immortality to light through the Gospel. *2 Timothy 1:10*

The power of the devil (Satan) is the third enemy. The devil's power is not to be laughed away. No one can measure the evil and misery the devil has brought about. Anger, hatred, unhappiness, greed—these are the devil's usual tools. His aim is to destroy all people. It is a relief to know that Jesus has redeemed us from the devil's power. God planned that Jesus would battle Satan.

> ✠ The reason the Son of God appeared was to destroy the works of the devil. *1 John 3:8b*

The Christian faith has an answer when people ask how Jesus could do all this.

He did *not* do it with silver and gold. Some people believe that money can do anything. Indeed, it can do much, but it cannot rescue a person from sin, death, and the power of the devil. Jesus paid a price higher than all the money in the world.

He willingly paid the price of His holy, precious blood. He was nailed to the cross. His blood flowed into the dust of Calvary's hill. It was holy blood because Jesus Himself is without sin. It was precious blood because it was the blood of the Son of God.

Through the ages Christians have believed this news of salvation through Jesus' sacrifice. They have especially loved the way Isaiah wrote about it in the 53d chapter of his prophecy:

> ✠ Surely He has borne our griefs and carried our sorrows; yet we esteemed Him stricken, smitten by God, and afflicted. But He was wounded for our transgressions, He was bruised for our iniquities; upon Him was the chastisement that made us whole, and with His stripes we are healed. *Isaiah 53:4-5*

136

THE CHRISTIAN BELIEVES: Jesus Has Redeemed Me

I must make sure to put myself into this picture. I am a sinner. Satan seeks to hold me in his power. Death threatens me.

Yet God loves me. Jesus' blood was shed for me. Jesus paid the price for my guilt. God has given me the Savior I need.

As a redeemed person I know that God will always care for me. I know also that He wants me to share the Good News with others.

Prayer Thought—

My salvation is freely given by God. Jesus
has done it all for me. My prayer, then,
is all of gratitude and praise for His
mercy to me.

Blest is the man, forever blest,
Whose guilt is pardoned by his God,
Whose sins with sorrow are confessed
And covered with his Savior's blood.

How glorious is that righteousness
That hides and cancels all his sins,
While bright the evidence of grace
Through all his life appears and shines!

Hymn 392, stanzas 1 and 4

137

27

Prophet, Priest, and King

"Christ" is from a Greek word which means "anointed one." To anoint is to pour a little pure oil on someone's head in a solemn ceremony. In ancient times people were anointed to show that they were *chosen* for a special calling. Kings and priests were anointed when they began their work. In some countries kings and queens are still anointed on the day they are crowned.

Jesus Christ is God's "Chosen One." It is natural to ask for what work Jesus was chosen.

Christians have searched Scriptures to discover what Jesus means to the world. Many titles can be applied to Him. He is Lord, Savior, Friend, Teacher, Guide. These and many other names are used in poems and hymns to describe Jesus.

Many Christians find it helpful to think of Jesus as our Prophet, Priest, and King. These three titles help us understand the work Jesus was chosen to do.

THIS IS THE CHRISTIAN FAITH: Jesus Shows Himself as Prophet, Priest, and King

Jesus' followers see Him as a prophet sent from God.

A prophet is a teacher. Sometimes, it is true, prophets foretold coming events, but their main job was to teach the ways and will of God.

When Jesus lived on this earth, He was often teaching. He was a popular teacher. He could speak about God and heaven from His own experience. Also, He explained things about God in stories easy to understand. Other teachers of religion knew *about* God. Jesus was one with the heavenly Father, as John writes:

> No one has ever seen God; the only Son, who is in the bosom of the Father, He has made Him known. *John 1:18*

Jesus is *still* the Teacher of Christians. He does not teach directly, as He did in Galilee or Jerusalem. However, when men teach in the church, they read and talk about Jesus' words in the Bible. The very idea of having a church with teachers and pastors comes from Jesus. He arranged it so that others would go on teaching His Word after His ascent into heaven. Men who faithfully teach Jesus' words have His authority. He said to the apostles:

> He who hears you hears Me, and he who rejects you rejects Me, and he who rejects Me rejects Him who sent Me. *Luke 10:16*

Besides being our Prophet, Jesus is our Priest.

A priest is one who makes offerings or sacrifices. In the Old Testament we read of priests who killed animals and burned them on stone altars. They carried bowls of blood to sprinkle in a room which they called the Holy Place. The sacrifices and blood foreshadowed the coming of the Lamb of God, the great Sacrifice for the sins of all people. The Scriptures tell us that Jesus was a priest who sacrificed Himself, saying:

> He entered once for all into the Holy Place, taking not the blood of goats and calves but His own blood, thus securing an eternal redemption. *Hebrews 9:12*

A priest also intercedes for others. That is, he prays for them or talks to God for all of them. Being the perfect Son of God, God Incarnate, Jesus is an excellent priest, the perfect Mediator (Go-Between), to speak to God for us. He paid the penalty for our sins. No one needs to be afraid

139

to face God with such a friend. John calls Him our "Advocate":

> ... if any one does sin, we have an advocate with the Father, Jesus Christ the Righteous.
> *1 John 2:1*

The Prophet-Priest is also a King.

Few countries today have kings. Once many nations had kings. Good kings governed for the happiness of their people. They made laws. They defended the people, and they provided for them.

Christians call Jesus King because He created and rules the whole universe in wisdom. True, not all people obey Jesus. Finally, in ways we may not understand, His will is done.

Jesus is King because He is Head of the church. The church is made up of all those whom God's Spirit has called by the Gospel. In faith these people call Him Lord.

Jesus is King because He is the Ruler of all who live in heaven. In heaven the greatest joy will be to praise Him and do His will. Christians agree with St. Paul:

> The Lord will rescue me from every evil and save me for His heavenly kingdom.
> *2 Timothy 4:18*

THE CHRISTIAN BELIEVES: Jesus Is My Prophet, Priest, and King

Jesus is my Teacher. All my life it will be important that I learn from Him. Since He is my Teacher, I will be His pupil. I will seek opportunities to study His words and hear them explained.

Jesus is my Priest. He sacrificed His holy blood for me. He was slain to make me acceptable to God. He is my Advocate. He pleads for me before His Father.

Jesus is my King. He is my Ruler because He made me. More than that, He is my King because He loved me and redeemed me. He makes me able to obey Him. Forever and ever I will praise and serve Him in heaven.

I pray that the Holy Spirit will open my
eyes to see all that Jesus means to me.
I pray for a mind ready to learn of my
Prophet, a heart ready to trust in my
Priest, and a will ready to trust my King.

Jesus, my Shepherd, Guardian, Friend,
My Prophet, Priest, and King,
My Lord, my Life, my Way, my End,
Accept the praise I bring.

Weak is the effort of my heart
And cold my warmest thought;
But when I see Thee as Thou art,
I'll praise Thee as I ought.

Hymn 364, stanzas 5 and 6

28

That I May Be His Own

A group of travelers listened to a guide tell about the building of the Egyptian pyramids. They marvelled as he explained how slaves moved the huge stone blocks with crude tools. They gasped in horror to hear that thousands of slaves died while building the pyramids.

At the end of his talk the guide asked, "Any questions?" One man had a question. He asked simply, "Why?" The guide stammered. "Why? Well, I suppose it was all to build a huge graveyard in which to bury dead kings." So lofty a project had such a lowly purpose.

When Christians study the life and work of Christ, they also may ask, "Why?" Why did God meet human misery with the salvation of the cross? Why did God's Son pour out His holy and precious blood? Why this sacrifice by God? Here is the answer from the meaning of the *Second Article.*

All this He has done that I may be His own, live under Him in His kingdom, and serve Him in everlasting righteousness, innocence, and blessedness, just as He is risen from the dead and lives and rules eternally. This is most certainly true.

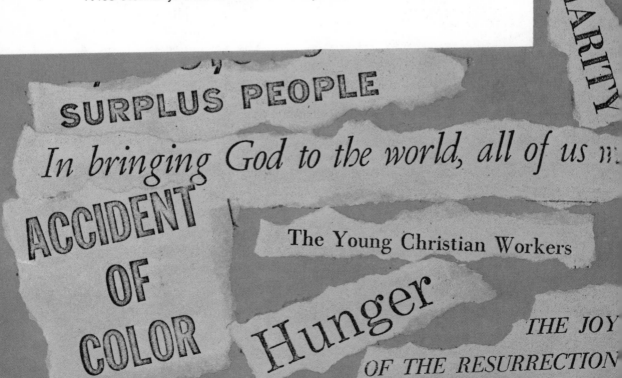

CHARITY

SURPLUS PEOPLE

In bringing God to the world, all of us n

ACCIDENT OF COLOR

The Young Christian Workers

Hunger

THE JOY OF THE RESURRECTION

All this He has done that I may be His own and live under Him in His kingdom. Jesus suffered and died to become our Lord. When we are born, Satan is our master. Sin keeps us slaves of Satan. By ourselves we can never escape. We are captives and able to do only those things which Satan wants. The prospect of death at the end of the road frightens us.

On the cross Jesus paid the debt of all people's sins. In His death He destroyed the power of Satan as the master of human beings. When the Holy Spirit causes us to believe in Jesus and His work for us, our sins are forgiven. We are moved out of Satan's power and under the rulership of Jesus. Death becomes the door to eternal life. St. Paul describes this move:

> He has delivered us from the dominion of darkness and transferred us to the kingdom of His beloved Son, in whom we have redemption, the forgiveness of sins.
> *Colossians 1:13-14*

God brings people to faith in Jesus. Through the ages, by God's grace sinful people are being "transferred . . . to the kingdom of His beloved Son." All these people belong to God. They are "God's nation." Some of His nation are still living in this world. Some left this world long ago to be with Jesus. Jesus did His work as Savior to have a people like this, of whom He could be the Lord. The Scriptures say it in the words:

> To this end Christ died and lived again, that He might be Lord both of the dead and of the living.
> *Romans 14:9*

This is why I was born, and why I have come into the world: to bear witness to the truth.

Christ

A TOUCH OF LOVE

A Christian spirit

The quality of mercy

give ourselves totally

The kingdom of Christ is a busy kingdom. Jesus did not die just to have His followers sit around and wait to go to heaven. He has set them apart to do His work. The catechism says that Jesus has purchased and won us for His kingdom also that we might serve Him. St. Paul was talking about this when he explained to his young friend Titus:

> He gave Himself for us to redeem us from all iniquity and to purify for Himself a people of His own who are zealous for good deeds.
>
> *Titus 2:14*

Christ has much work in this world. There are hungry people to be fed. Someone has said that more than half the people of the world go to bed hungry every night. There are sick people to be cared for. People with breaking hearts need someone to lift them from despair. The whole world needs to hear about Jesus' love. Who will do all this? There is enough misery and grief in the world to keep God's people busy night and day.

Christians have been busy night and day for hundreds of years. All over the world they are busy at Jesus' work right now. They build hospitals and schools. They gather the orphans. They send boatloads of food for the starving. They tramp to desert or to jungle to carry the good news of God's love in Christ. They continue to pour out their money, their energy, and sometimes even their lives. Jesus came to serve. His people know that they are put under Him to be His servants and do His work. Wherever a Christian is comforting or healing or teaching or feeding or helping, he is doing the work for which Christ has saved him.

God's people serve in *righteousness*. They are not sinless. But they daily pray for forgiveness. God forgives them for Jesus' sake, and they seek to serve Him with godly lives.

In *innocence* God's people serve Him. God makes them new creatures who want to follow the perfect example of Jesus. He daily assures them in His Word that their guilt is lifted.

In *blessedness* God's people serve Him. They are happy because they know they belong to God. In life devoted to God and His work the redeemed find deep joy, contentment, and fulfillment.

Christians do not doubt that Jesus is a king. He died on the cross, but He also rose again. He lives! He is alive to rule His people as He calls them through the church and its preaching. Because He lives, nothing will ever stop our joy in calling Jesus Lord. Not even death can halt it. After death God's people go on to serve Him everlastingly in heaven.

THE CHRISTIAN BELIEVES: God Has Accepted Me to Serve Him

On my own, I certainly do not deserve to be a servant of God. Because of what Jesus has done, God accepts me. I know that this means I will live with Him forever. I am freed from slavery to Satan.

I am glad that I am God's servant. With all of God's people, He has work for me to do. I prepare myself to be a good workman for Him. I am alert to see what part of His work He assigns to me every day. No matter what earthly calling I may follow, I know that I am first of all God's child and God's servant.

Prayer Thought—

I pray that my eyes will be opened every day to see what has happened to me because Jesus died for me. I ask God to help me understand my calling as a servant of His kingdom. I seek His guidance to know what work He wants me to do for Him from day to day.

May the dear blood once shed for me
My blest atonement prove
That I from first to last may be
The purchase of Thy love!

Let every thought and work and word
To Thee be ever given;
Then life shall be Thy service, Lord,
And death the gate of heaven.

Hymn 336, stanzas 4 and 5

145

29

The Holy Spirit

If you tell an artist to draw a picture of the Holy Spirit what will you get? He may draw you a dove. Or perhaps he'll draw tongues of fire. He doesn't try to portray this Person of the Holy Trinity in any kind of human form.

Our curiosity is aroused. The Bible does say that the Holy Spirit appeared as a dove at Jesus' baptism. It also says that the Holy Spirit's presence was seen in what looked like candle flames or tongues of fire on the disciples' heads. It says that He came on the first Pentecost with the sound of a rushing wind.

We're up against a mystery. Questions crowd our minds. Who is the Holy Spirit? What is His main work? What does He do in us?

We start right here: the Holy Spirit is the Third Person of the Holy Trinity. He is God. He is part of God's plan and work for us. He comes from the Father and the Son. He comes in answer to a promise of Jesus: "I will send the Counselor."

THIS IS THE CHRISTIAN FAITH: God Comes to His People as the Holy Spirit

Why do we call this Person "Ghost" in the Creeds? Ghost here means spirit. A spirit is a person who lives but who does not have a body. He is invisible. So the Holy Ghost is a real person. Yet He has and needs no body.

Why do we call this Person the *Holy* Spirit? He is not just an ordinary spirit. To be holy means to be set apart. The Holy Spirit *is* set apart— in fact, He *is* God. He is perfect and completely righteous. As God He is all powerful, all knowing and everywhere and always present. Many of the things we say about God the Father and about Christ we say also about the Holy Spirit.

Is "Holy Spirit" just another name for God? The Father, the Son, and the Holy Spirit are all one God. They are the three Persons of the Holy Trinity. The Holy Spirit is one with the Father and the Son. Yet He is different. Each Person in the triune God does some special work for us. We can see this most clearly when we remember that only Jesus suffered and died for us. The Holy Spirit has His own special work to do for us. We will discuss His work in a separate lesson. We do need to remember that the Holy Spirit is God *with* the Father and the Son.

After Jesus returned to heaven, He sent the Holy Spirit to His church as He had promised. In making that promise, Jesus had called the Holy Spirit "Counselor."

> ✠ But when the Counselor comes, whom I shall send to you from the Father, even the Spirit of truth, who proceeds from the Father, He will bear witness to Me. *John 15:26*

The disciples of Jesus experienced the coming of the Holy Spirit on Pentecost. This was 50 days after Easter and 10 days after Jesus had gone back to heaven. On that day the sound as of a wind and little flames as of fire on the apostles' heads revealed that the Holy Spirit was there. The Holy Spirit doesn't appear in that way today. He comes through the hearing and reading and teaching of the Gospel. He comes through Baptism and the Lord's Supper.

No one can be a believer until the Holy Spirit comes to him. Paul told his friends in Corinth:

> ✠ No one can say "Jesus is Lord" except by the Holy Spirit. *1 Corinthians 12:3b*

The more we learn about the Holy Ghost, the more we appreciate Him. His *name* may puzzle us at first. However, what we learn about Him makes us eager to get better acquainted.

What do Christians believe about the Holy Spirit? They believe that He is God. St. Paul says, "God's Spirit dwells in you" (1 Corinthians 3:16). Christians believe that He is close at hand, no matter where they are. David knew he could not find a place where the Holy Spirit could not be. He asked, "Whither shall I go from Thy Spirit?" (Psalm 139:7). Christians believe that the Holy Spirit dwells in their hearts and never leaves them. They believe that Jesus has kept His promise: "I will pray the Father, and He will give you another Counselor to be with you forever, even the Spirit of truth." (John 14:16-17a)

THE CHRISTIAN BELIEVES: My God Comes to Me as the Holy Spirit

What a wonderful God I have! I can read in the Bible of His great deeds to people far away and long ago. Yet He is not a distant stranger to me. He is close and near and dear to me today. He dwells right in my heart.

As a sinner I cannot praise God adequately. But God made a new relationship when He sent Jesus. Having cleansed me of my sin, my God lives in me. I am happy to confess with my fellow believers: "I believe in the Holy Ghost."

Prayer Thought—

I ask God to send the Holy Spirit to me daily. Because the Spirit comes to me through the Gospel, I pray that I may be led to faithful study of the Word. I ask God to help me live always as a person in whose heart the Holy Spirit has made His home.

O Holy Spirit, enter in
And in our hearts Thy work begin,
Thy temple deign to make us;
Sun of the soul, Thou Light Divine,
Around and in us brightly shine,
To joy and gladness wake us
That we, in Thee
Truly living, To Thee giving
Prayer unceasing,
May in love be still increasing.

Hymn 235, stanza 1

30

The Holy Spirit at Work in Me

What are the great deeds of the Holy Spirit? Especially, what does He do for people? And does He do anything for me? These are all fair questions. God's people have found answers in the Scriptures.

Christians confess their faith in the Holy Ghost. In explaining that faith, they think at once of the Spirit's work. They believe He exists, and they also believe that without Him they would not be Christians. They may express this faith in the words of the *Third Article.*

SANCTIFICATION

I believe in the Holy Ghost; the holy Christian church, the communion of saints; the forgiveness of sins; the resurrection of the body; and the life everlasting. Amen.

What does this mean?

I believe that I cannot by my own understanding or effort believe in Jesus Christ, my Lord, or come to Him. But the Holy Spirit has called me through the Gospel, enlightened me with His gifts, and sanctified and kept me in true faith. In the same way He calls, gathers, enlightens, and sanctifies the whole Christian church on earth, and keeps it united with Jesus Christ in the one true faith.

THIS IS THE CHRISTIAN FAITH: The Holy Spirit Works for Man's Salvation

Human beings can do remarkable things by their own understanding and effort. They can orbit the earth in spacecraft. They can change the course of a river. They can travel in a submarine under the polar ice cap. But one thing they cannot do.

By his own understanding and effort no one can believe in Jesus as Lord or come to Him. At birth sinful man does not have God's Spirit living in him to move him to love and trust God. The Scriptures point out how helpless men are regarding God:

> The unspiritual man does not receive the gifts of the Spirit of God, for they are folly to him, and he is not able to understand them because they are spiritually discerned. *1 Corinthians 2:14*

St. Paul says it in simple words:

> No one can say "Jesus is Lord" except by the Holy Spirit.
> *1 Corinthians 12:3b*

This is where the work of the Holy Spirit fits in. Without Jesus and His work for us, we are forever lost from God. But we cannot believe in Jesus without the Holy Spirit's work. The Holy Spirit does several things for us.

He *calls* people. He brings them the good news that Jesus died and rose again for them. He calls by telling them that Jesus wants them for His own people.

The Spirit calls *through the Gospel.* He uses the Gospel to get His invitation to people. Perhaps a mother or a Sunday school teacher tells a child about Jesus. That is the Holy Spirit calling the child. A pastor preaches. The Holy Spirit is calling the congregation. Sometimes it is

a book or a radio program or television drama that tells the Gospel. Whenever the Gospel is told, the Holy Spirit is calling. St. Paul knew that the Spirit would work through the letters he was writing:

> [God] called you through our Gospel so that you may obtain the glory of our Lord Jesus Christ. *2 Thessalonians 2:14*

Jesus told the story of the wedding supper of the prince (Matthew 22:1-10). People were *invited* to the supper. Without the invitation they could not have come. This is the first work of the Spirit—to invite people to take what God offers.

The Holy Spirit also *enlightens* us with His gifts. If we believe in Jesus as our Savior, this enlightening has happened to us. It keeps right on happening. Without the Holy Spirit we do not know how much we need a Savior. We can't see how bad sin really is. Or if we see the evil of sin, we can't see our Savior. The Spirit turns on the light. When He does, we see our sin *and* our Savior. Light is good. When the Holy Spirit enlightens us, we see what God has done for us and we can have real hope. The Bible tells us that Paul prayed for this gift for his friends:

> ✠ May the God of hope fill you with all joy and peace in believing, so that by the power of the Holy Spirit you may abound in hope.
> *Romans 15:13*

The Holy Spirit also *sanctifies* the believers in the true faith. To sanctify means to make holy. The Holy Spirit makes people holy by putting true faith into their hearts. They accept Jesus as Savior. Their sins are forgiven. God then sees them without sin—as holy. He assures us:

> In Christ Jesus you are all sons of God through faith. For as many of you as were baptized into Christ have put on Christ.
> *Galatians 3:26-27*

The Holy Spirit makes people different. Because they are Christians, they do things that please God. The Holy Spirit helps them do good works. Christians can say:

> We are His workmanship, created in Christ Jesus for good works.
> *Ephesians 2:10a*

The Holy Spirit also *keeps* believers in the true faith. There is danger that they may fall away. Satan tries to lure them from the faith. Even friends tempt them. Christians know that to lose faith in Jesus is the worst thing that can happen. They take comfort in God's promise:

> ✠ You . . . are guarded through faith for a salvation ready to be revealed in the last time.
> *1 Peter 1:5*

THE CHRISTIAN BELIEVES: By the Holy Spirit I Am God's Child

I am the result of this wonderful work of God's Spirit. He calls me. He enlightens me by the Word. He sanctifies me. I trust Him to keep me in the true faith by advising, warning, cheering, and strengthening me.

His work makes me humble. By myself I would be lost. I would be so ignorant of God that I would not even know I was lost. I need the Holy Spirit's work in me constantly. Therefore I will seek Him by keeping close to the Gospel. In the Gospel I know He will find me and keep working in my heart throughout my life.

Prayer Thought—

I wish to remain God's child. I wish to do His will. I am grateful for the Holy Spirit. I sincerely ask God to send His Holy Spirit to me always, that I may remain a true believer.

My Comforter, give power
That I may stand secure
When in temptation's hour
The world and sin allure.
The Son to me revealing,
Inspire my thought and feeling,
His Word of grace to ponder,
Nor let me from Him wander.
On me Thy gifts and graces shower:
My Comforter, give power!

Hymn 335, stanza 3

153

31

The Holy Christian Church

How do you know what a new baby's name will be? The parents choose the first name and often a middle name. No one needs to make a choice about the last name. The baby gets the family name.

For a baby to be given life is a wonderful act of God. But God does not give babies the gift of life all by themselves. He places them into families.

For a person to become a child of God and to receive the gift of spiritual life is also a wonderful act of God. In this case too, God places the new Christian into the family of His people.

Christians thankfully confess that they are members of this family of God. In the *Third Article* of the Apostles' Creed they say:

> I believe in the holy Christian church, the communion of saints.

A Christian believes that what the Holy Spirit does for him is only one example of what goes on in many hearts. He confesses that the Holy Spirit

> calls, gathers, enlightens, and sanctifies the whole Christian church on earth, and keeps it united with Jesus Christ in the one true faith. . . .

THIS IS THE CHRISTIAN FAITH: God's Believers Are Bound Together in the Church

The word *church* is used in a number of senses. It may refer to a building or a local congregation; it may be used for a denomination, such as the Lutheran.

When we say we believe in the holy Christian church, we refer to the church as people.

The church is not just *any* people. About three billion people live on this earth. Some of them are the church, and some are not. You can't tell whether a person belongs to God's family by the color of his skin or the shape of his eyes. The language he speaks or the country he calls his home have nothing to do with it. Some of the people who are the church are rich, while others are poor. Some are young and some old. Some are women or girls, others men or boys. Some are well educated, and some can't even read.

We understand what the church is when we remember that the Holy Spirit gathers the church. He calls people into the church by what He does for them and to them.

The church is made up of sinful people, people who know and admit that they are sinners. They are sorry for their sins. They believe that Jesus, God's Son, died to take away their sins. They accept the mercy that God has given them in His Son. St. Peter explains that God's *mercy* puts people into a new relationship with God. He says:

> Once you were no people, but now you are God's people; once you had not received mercy, but now you have received mercy.
>
> *1 Peter 2:10*

We know that God wants all people to receive His mercy. Jesus died for all people. God holds out forgiveness of sins to all. He sincerely invites everyone to be among His people.

Some people believe and accept God's offer. Others do not accept it. Those who do accept and believe have only the Holy Spirit to thank.

That is why we say that it is the Holy Spirit who gathers the church. As He brings people to faith, they become part of the church. The church, then, is a body of people who have a special characteristic. They believe that Jesus is their Savior. This group of people we may call Jesus' body, as Paul does when he writes:

> He [Jesus] is the Head of the body, the church. *Colossians 1:18a*

155

A word which is translated "church" means "those who have been called out." From the people of the world, Christians have been called out to be God's own people. God alone knows how many there are. They are all over the world. It is impossible to count them.

This body of people, the church, is holy. It is holy because the people are cleansed of their sins. By the Holy Spirit working in them they are also able to lead lives pleasing to God. The Holy Spirit helps them keep away from unholy living.

The church is called "Christian." It exists because of what Jesus Christ has done as Savior. It is therefore called by His name.

The Father, Son, and Holy Spirit work to make sinful people become the church. St. Paul explains:

> ✠ For through Him we both have access in one Spirit to the Father. So then you are no longer strangers and sojourners, but you are fellow citizens with the saints and members of the household of God.
> *Ephesians 2:18-19*

THE CHRISTIAN BELIEVES: I Am a Member of God's Family

As a believer I am God's child. But I am not the only child of God. Many others have become children of God. They are all my brothers and sisters in Christ. Together we make up the church. Whenever I think about the church and what it should be doing, I include myself. I am bound together with all Christians to be the body of Christ and to do His work.

Prayer Thought—

I thank God again for calling me to faith. But especially I thank Him for placing me into His family. I ask Him to make me aware that I am in the church. I pray that He will guide me to be a useful member of His household.

Lord Jesus, Thou the Church's Head,
Thou art her one Foundation;
In Thee she trusts, before Thee bows,
And waits for Thy salvation.
Built on this Rock secure,
Thy Church shall endure
E'en though the world decay
And all things pass away.
Oh, hear, oh, hear us, Jesus!

Hymn 477, stanza 1

157

32

Where Is the Church?

The holy Christian church is the whole number of people who believe in Jesus as their Lord and Savior.

In one way the church is invisible. No one but God can look into another person's heart. He alone can tell whether a person is truly a believer. The Lord knows every one of His people. For human beings the church is uncountable, but the people who are the church are real, visible people.

In another way, however, we *can* find the church. Christians believe that God has given certain marks to identify the church.

God has told us the secret of how He works to call people to believe in Him. He says that wherever His Word is taught, there some people will believe it. He has clothed this wonderful promise in a lovely word picture:

> ✠ For as the rain and the snow come down from heaven and return not thither but water the earth, making it bring forth and sprout, giving seed to the sower and bread to the eater, so shall My Word be that goes forth from My mouth; it shall not return to Me empty, but it shall accomplish that which I purpose and prosper in the thing for which I sent it.
> *Isaiah 55:10-11*

Imagine what these words must mean, for instance, to a missionary. He may be working where no one has ever taught the Gospel before. He might well wonder, "Is the church here?" He sees nothing to show the presence of the church. There are no buildings with arched windows and stained glass. There are no crosses. No Bibles lie on the tables in the homes, and Jesus' picture is not on the walls. No billboards urge people to go to church. One might say, "I doubt whether the church is here. I see none of the usual things that remind one of the church."

Church buildings and equipment do not prove that the church is present. Anyone could put up buildings with stained glass and crosses and organs.

The church is present where believers are. Therefore the missionary takes heart when he remembers God's promise. He says, "I am teaching God's Word here. Therefore there are believers here. The church *is* here."

Wherever believers are, they soon begin to get together. God wants them to. They seek one another out. A Christian does not want to be the church all by himself. Far back in Old Testament days, people who came to believe in the true God found one another. Malachi tells about believers getting together:

> ✠ Those who feared the Lord spoke with one another; the Lord heeded and heard them, and a book of remembrance was written before Him of those who feared the Lord and thought on His name. *Malachi 3:16*

In those days, and ever since, people come to "fear the Lord" when the Word of God is taught. Since New Testament times people have been baptized in the name of the true God, and have shared the Sacrament of the Altar. When these believers assemble, they become the church in that place.

Malachi says, "Those who feared the Lord spoke with one another." God's people are always eager to tell others—anyone who will listen—what they believe. From the very beginning of the New Testament church, Christians were ready even to put statements of their faith into writing. That is why we have creeds. The Apostles' Creed is one of the oldest statements of the Christian faith.

Whenever we find a group of people who seem to be teaching religion, we have a right to ask, "Are you the church?" They can answer by telling us what they believe. More often they may hand us a book or a written statement. They may say, "Here is our confessional standard." That is another way of saying, "Here is what we believe and confess." The statements are sometimes long, sometimes short. So that others may learn more fully what they believe, groups of Christians have often prepared very long statements of their faith.

By sharing and comparing statements of faith, God's people in many parts of the world have found one another. Sometimes they have had to correct those who wandered away from the Bible teaching. This process of finding others who believe God's Word and accept Jesus as Savior is still going on. Little groups join to form larger groups. They keep on seeking so that all of God's people may be one in mind and heart.

THE CHRISTIAN BELIEVES: As a Believer in the Gospel I Am in the Church

The first question I ask about the church is not: "Are others in the church?" First I ask, "Am I in the church?" I do not take pride in discovering that my church is "right" and others are "wrong." My first concern is to study and ask God to keep me strong in faith. As I believe God's Word I will be in the church.

I will also gladly share my faith. I will rejoice to find others who believe God's promises in Jesus. I will be grateful that God places me in a group of Christians where I can both learn and teach more and more of God's message. It is not a distasteful task to work with my fellow Christians. It is a joy and a privilege. Through other members of the church, God has brought His Gospel to me. I need my fellow Christians. And I can serve to pass on the Gospel to others. As I look down the long list of people who are God's disciples in all ages, I am excited. By God's grace my name, too, is in the "book of remembrance" written before God of those who fear the Lord and think on His name.

Prayer Thought—

Before I pray, I may prepare by thinking of all the Christians I know and by remembering what they have meant to me. Then I will thank God for making me a member of His church. I will ask Him to strengthen me by His Word to help bring others close to His Word and into the church.

I love Thy kingdom, Lord,
The house of Thine abode,
The Church our blest Redeemer saved
With His own precious blood.

I love Thy Church, O God.
Her walls before Thee stand,
Dear as the apple of Thine eye
And graven on Thy hand.

Hymn 462, stanzas 1 and 2

33

The Broken Church

Why are there so many different kinds of churches?
That question bothers many people. It is confusing, especially to a young Christian, to discover so many different "brands" of Christianity. The different church groups all claim to be right. Some people brush off the whole question by deciding that none of the churches is right. They use that as an excuse to stay away from all churches.

It is a sorry sight to see the church of Jesus divided. It is important to know something about how it came to be divided. Even more important are the efforts to bring all Christians back to agreement.

THIS IS THE CHRISTIAN FAITH: Submitting to God's Word Unites Christians

We are sure that Jesus did not intend His followers to be divided. Not long before He died on the cross He prayed to His Father:

> The glory which Thou hast given Me I have given to them, that they may be one even as We are one. *John 17:22*

Jesus knew that those who believed in Him would be separated from unbelievers. But He did not want them to be separated from each other. To keep them all believing and teaching the same truths, He gave them His Word through the Holy Spirit. The Spirit guided the apostles to write God's truth for all to read. This Word was to draw them together even while it separated them from the unbelievers of the world. Jesus said:

> I have given them Thy Word, and the world has hated them because they are not of the world, even as I am not of the world. *John 17:14*

It is not surprising to find Christians disagreeing about many things. They are of all ages and countries and conditions. Differences in dress, language, food, and customs are not wrong. God's family includes all kinds of interesting people.

However, already when Jesus was on earth some of His followers began to believe and teach differences that *did* matter. They took ideas from their own minds and pretended that they were God's truth. Soon others began to believe them. Jesus called such teachers "false prophets" and warned against them. He said:

> Beware of false prophets, who come to you in sheep's clothing but inwardly are ravenous wolves. *Matthew 7:15*

Some people who teach false doctrine may do so deliberately. They know the truth but reject it. For instance, some knew that a sinner can be saved only by trusting in Jesus and His saving work. Yet they taught that a person can be accepted by God for doing certain good deeds.

Others have taught and believed false doctrines because they did not know any better. They believed false prophets without checking their words with what God says. Sometimes they just did not study God's

163

Word carefully enough. In these ways many different teachings and church groups came to be.

How are we to deal with the problem of many differing teachings? First, if a man *knows* what God says and still rejects it, we stay away from him. St. Paul warns:

> ✠ Take note of those who create dissensions and difficulties in opposition to the doctrine which you have been taught; avoid them.
>
> *Romans 16:17*

However, if people say they want to know and believe what God says, we can act differently. We do not agree with their mistakes, but we do not forget that if they believe in Jesus as their Lord and Savior, they are fellow Christians. To such people we can talk and with them study God's Word. In this way God's people can help one another to know and believe God's truths.

Sometimes individual Christians help each other in this way. Sometimes leaders of church groups meet to study God's Word. Gradually they may come to see what God says and to agree. This is pleasing to the Lord who wants one church. In His eyes all believers *are* one, though some may be weak or confused. Christians know that not their own ideas but God's clear Word must decide what they believe and teach. Jesus said about this:

> ✠ If you continue in My Word, you are truly My disciples, and you will know the truth, and the truth will make you free. *John 8:31-32*

THE CHRISTIAN BELIEVES: God Guides Me to Christian Fellowship by His Word

Jesus prayed so lovingly for His disciples and me just before He died. He prayed that we all might be one in His holy church.

I have done nothing to deserve being called to His holy Christian church.

164

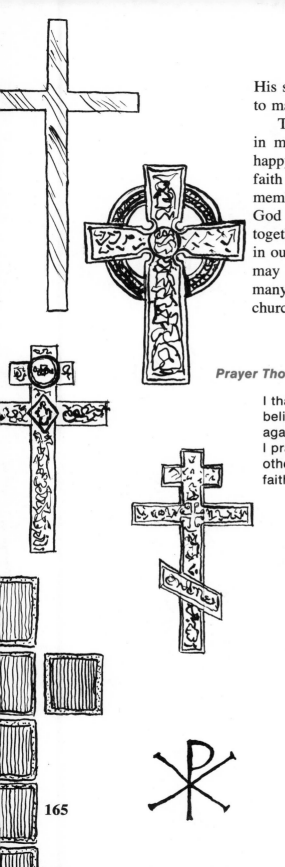

His steadfast love and mercy moved Him to make me His child.

This thought prompts me to be humble in my dealings with other people. I am happy to find others who confess their faith in God as I do. This is my joy in membership in my congregation. I praise God for the chance to study His Word together with my instructor and friends in our class. I pray that God's Holy Spirit may work through His Word to bring many more to the church. I pray that the church may be united in this world too.

Prayer Thought—

I thank God for leading me to know and believe His truth. I ask to be protected against the temptations of false teaching. I pray that I may be helpful in leading others to enjoy the blessings of sound faith.

Preserve Thy Word, O Savior,
To us this latter day
And let Thy kingdom flourish,
Enlarge Thy Church, we pray.
Oh, keep our faith from failing,
Keep hope's bright star aglow.
Let naught from Thy Word turn us
While wand'ring here below.

Hymn 264, stanza 1

165

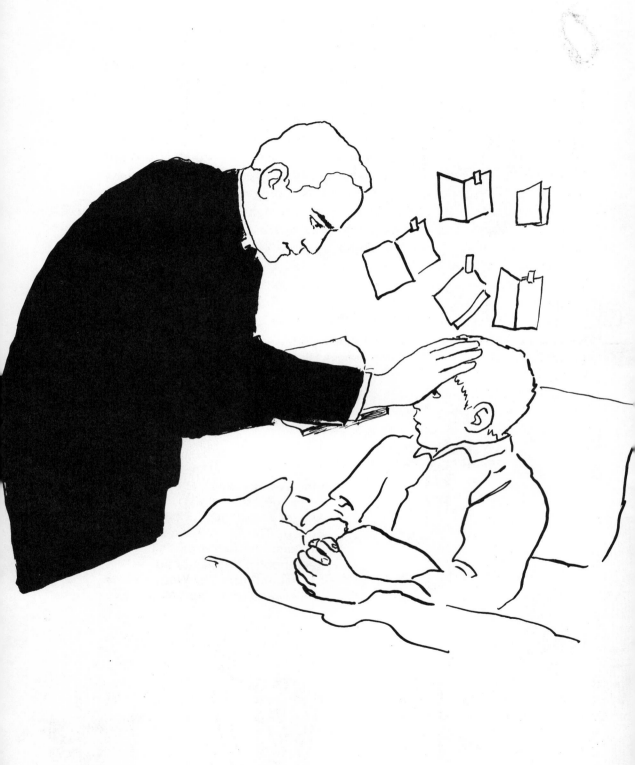

34

The Church in Action

You walk past a factory. What's going on inside? Trucks hustle in and out. Humming noises come from windows. Sparks leap into the sky. On the building is a sign, BETHLEHEM STEEL COMPANY. Men are making steel for cars and bridges and hundreds of other uses. That's industry in action.

You walk past an office building. It's much quieter. What's going on in there? Again a sign helps: SMITH AND ANDERSON — STOCK BROKERS. Inside is the rustle of paper work needed to gather the money to keep factories running. They sell and buy shares of great companies. That's business in action.

You walk past a church. What's going on in there? Perhaps the sign doesn't help much. It reads ST. JOHN'S LUTHERAN CHURCH or some other such name. You hear people singing and the full melody of an organ. A man talks. That's the church in action.

What is the action of the church? It's God's Holy Spirit at work among believers in the Gospel. Martin Luther indicates this in these words of the explanation of the *Third Article:*

> In this Christian church day after day He fully forgives my sins and the sins of all believers.

THIS IS THE CHRISTIAN FAITH: God Works in the Church to Give Forgiveness and Eternal Life

Perhaps it is better to compare the church to a hospital. What goes on in a hospital? People are healed of diseases and injuries. They are nursed back to health and strength.

In the church, people are healed of the worst disease of all — sin. Jesus' blood is the only thing that can cure a sinner and take away the death-dealing power of his sin. When he is healed of his sin, he feels and is new. Then he is ready to work and bring the same wonderful healing to others.

God has provided the healing forgiveness of sins for all people. He is anxious that all people know about it and believe it. He wants people to hear the message as St. Paul told it:

> ✠ Let it be known to you therefore, brethren, that through this Man forgiveness of sins is proclaimed to you, and by Him everyone that believes is freed from everything from which you could not be freed by the law of Moses. *Acts 13:38-39*

Christians believe that people come to believe in Jesus by the working of the Holy Spirit. The Holy Spirit works when the Gospel of Jesus' work for us is made known. To get this Good News to everyone is the work of the church.

Before He ascended into heaven, Jesus gave to His church its assignment. He told His people:

> ✠ Go therefore and make disciples of all nations, baptizing them in the name of the Father and of the Son and of the Holy Spirit, teaching them to observe all that I have commanded you; and lo, I am with you always, to the close of the age. *Matthew 28:19-20*

Jesus promised to be with His people "to the close of the age." The work for which they need His presence also is to go on to the end of this present world. When He returns in glory, the work of the church in this world will be completed.

Christians join together to reflect the loving concern of the heavenly Father for all men. God's people use radio and television to beam the good news of forgiveness over the airwaves. They operate publishing houses. They print Bibles and books and tracts. They send pastors to prisons and hospitals, and missionaries to faraway lands. They send chaplains to men in military service and to students in college. To the blind, the deaf, and the aged the good news of God's love goes out because the church is in action. God's people work in community projects to maintain hospitals and institutions of help.

Such great work requires that God's people be strong in faith. Therefore they keep on teaching themselves and the people they bring in. The Word of God builds weak Christians into strong Christians — and strong Christians into even stronger ones.

In schools and Sunday schools, in confirmation classes and vacation schools, God's people teach. In high schools and colleges, on vast campuses and in jungle huts, they teach. Always their teaching has one purpose — that the life of Christ may be formed in the heart of the believer.

What a busy workshop is the church in action!

THE CHRISTIAN BELIEVES: I Am Part of the Church in Action

As a member of the body of Christ, I have work to do. Jesus wants me to be active in telling the Good News, in teaching, and in learning.

This makes me realize how much I need my fellow Christians. All alone, I will not get much done for Christ. Together, millions of us Christians become a mighty force. We can join our prayers, our money, and our talents and become the church in action all over the world. We can be God's arms, God's voice, to bring the good news of God's forgiveness and everlasting hope to all men. I am part of a never-ending crusade.

Prayer Thought —

> I thank God that He forgives me day by day. I ask Him to give me wisdom and strength to see and do the work He asks me to do. I pray that I may be a worthy witness and worker for Jesus.

> Hark! the Church proclaims her honor,
> And her strength is only this:
> God hath laid His choice upon her,
> And the work she doth is His.
>
> Onward, then! For naught despairing,
> Calm we follow at His word,
> Thus through joy and sorrow bearing
> Faithful witness to our Lord.
>
> *Hymn 461, stanzas 1 and 4*

35

The Resurrection of the Body

When a person dies, a word that is spoken many times is "last." A person may say, "I want to look into the casket and see John's face for the *last* time." The trip to the cemetery is called the dead person's *"last* ride." The grave is spoken of as the *"last* resting place."

Right here the Christian faith completely disagrees. Christians do not believe that death is the last thing that happens to a human being.

The work of the Father, the Son, and the Holy Spirit has everything to do with what happens to a Christian after death. The wonderful result of all that God does for His people makes death not an end but really a beginning. And so the fear of death fades away for God's people because they believe with the *Third Article* that

> On the last day He will raise me and all the dead and give
> me and all believers in Christ eternal life.

THIS IS THE CHRISTIAN FAITH: God Will Raise
the Bodies of All Men

Sooner or later all people die. By disease or accident or just old age a person dies, and his body at once begins to decay. It must be put out of sight. Usually it is buried in the ground.

Death of the body is not the end of a person. The soul of the Christian shall always "be with the Lord" (1 Thessalonians 4:17). Of those who die believing in Jesus, Scripture says:

> Blessed are the dead who die in the Lord henceforth.
>
> *Revelation 14:13*

Those who die rejecting the forgiveness earned by Jesus are not blessed. Jesus tells them to depart from Him.

Christians look forward to Jesus' return in visible form. On that Day of the Lord a strange and wonderful thing will happen. All the bodies

170

of all people will come back to life. Jesus Himself foretold this when
He said:

> The hour is coming when all who are in the tombs will hear His voice
> and come forth, those who have done good to the resurrection of life
> and those who have done evil to the resurrection of judgment.
>
> *John 5:28-29*

God's idea of good and evil people is different from the usual idea
of men. All people have sinned. St. Paul says: "All have sinned and fall
short of the glory of God" (Romans 3:23). Some, however, have "washed
their robes and made them white in the blood of the Lamb" (Revelation
7:14b). That is a figurative way of saying that God has removed guilt
from these sinners and given them life.

God has already raised some people from the dead. He raised Jairus'
daughter (Matthew 9:25). He raised the son of the widow of Nain
(Luke 7:15). He raised Lazarus (John 11:44). Jesus Himself, of course,
came out of the grave after He had been killed.

The bodies of believers will be raised in glory on Resurrection Day.
Jesus asked His friends to examine Him carefully when He came back
to life. "Touch Me," He said, "and make sure it is really Myself and not
a stranger who looks like Me."

171

Yet the bodies of God's people will be changed. The Holy Spirit will glorify our bodies. St. Paul explains this in words of hope which are read over the grave when Christians are buried:

> So it is with the resurrection of the dead. What is sown is perishable; what is raised is imperishable. It is sown in dishonor; it is raised in glory. It is sown in weakness; it is raised in power.
>
> *1 Corinthians 15:42-43*

We do not know exactly what it will be like to have such a "glorified body." We get a hint when God promises:

> ✠ [He] will change our lowly body to be like His glorious body, by the power which enables Him even to subject all things to Himself.
>
> *Philippians 3:21*

As Jesus' body was the same, yet changed, so will the bodies of believers be. We can be certain that our glorified bodies will be suitable in every way.

The bodies of unbelievers will not be glorified. They will join the souls in everlasting punishment.

St. Peter predicted that many would scoff at this teaching. Unbelievers still say: "When you're dead you're dead." Why, then, are Christians so certain that they will be raised?

Christians trust Jesus. They trust His power. They trust His words of promise. He promised directly:

✠ For this is the will of My Father, that everyone who sees the Son and believes in Him should have eternal life; and I will raise him up at the Last Day. *John 6:40*

THE CHRISTIAN BELIEVES: I Will Rise from Death by Jesus' Power

When I die, trusting in my Savior, Christ will take my soul into His keeping. When the Day of Resurrection comes, the Holy Spirit will raise my body.

Death is still mysterious to me. When Satan tries to frighten me by thoughts of death, I remember my Lord as the Conqueror of death. In Him I have victory over death.

Prayer Thought—

> I thank God that He has taken the sting
> from death for me and all believers.
> I pray God to keep me strong in faith all
> my life. I ask that when I die I may still
> be trusting in Christ. I pray that my body
> may be raised from death to eternal life
> for Jesus' sake.

I am flesh and must return
Unto dust, whence I am taken;
But by faith I now discern
That from death I shall awaken
With my Savior to abide
In His glory, at His side.

Glorified, I shall anew
With this flesh then be enshrouded;
In this body I shall view
God, my Lord, with eyes unclouded;
In this flesh I then shall see
Jesus Christ eternally.

Hymn 206, stanzas 4 and 5

173

36

Eternal Life

God's people are not at home in this world.

To be sure, most of them enjoy a happy earthly home. They appreciate this as a gift of God. They also may love and show loyalty to the country in which they live.

Yet a child of God believes that he does not belong to this world. He is passing through. Like the believers in Old Testament times, he calls himself a stranger and an exile on the earth.

If this earth is not home for a Christian, there must be a different home.

That is exactly what Christians confess when they say that they believe in "the life everlasting." They not only believe that this everlasting life exists, but they also believe that it exists *for them.* Christ has earned it for all who will accept it. That is why Christians explain their faith in everlasting life by saying in the *Third Article* that the Holy Spirit will "give . . . me and all believers in Christ eternal life."

THIS IS THE CHRISTIAN FAITH: Eternal Life Is the
Final Goal of God's People

Christians often use the name "heaven" when speaking of this eternal life. When we hear that word, questions crowd into our minds. We soon find that God does not fully answer all these questions now but He does give us some glimpses of heaven. He tells us all we need to know. For the rest we say, "Trust God and wait patiently."

Again and again Scripture reports God's wonderful promises about eternal life. Jesus clearly explained that His work as Savior was to give this gift to men:

> This is the will of the Father, that everyone who sees the Son and believes in Him should have eternal life.   *John 6:40*

Jesus called Himself the Good Shepherd who provides the green pastures of eternal life for His followers:

> ✻ My sheep hear My voice, and I know them, and they follow Me; and

174

> I give them eternal life, and they shall never perish, and no one shall snatch them out of My hand.
> *John 10:27-28*

Eternal life is only for believers in Christ. Sin brings death, which is the opposite of life. No person can live forever unless he gets rid of the death-dealing disease of sin. He cannot live forever unless God's own life-power is in him. Only Jesus can rid us of sin. This He did when He died on the cross. Only the Holy Spirit can put God's life-power into us. This He does through Baptism and the proclamation of the Gospel. For the believer in Christ, death is destroyed and life is given, the life we get through our faith in Jesus and which begins in this world and goes on forever.

For God's people, then, what is everlasting life?

It means to live with God. St. Paul looked forward to it, knowing that life with Christ would follow his farewell to the world, He said:

> ✠ My desire is to depart and be with Christ. *Philippians 1:23*

It means to live without the pain and sorrow we suffer in this world. It means to enjoy a life of perfection and joy as God originally intended human beings to live. It is not possible to imagine the wonders of heaven. When we try, we decide with St. Paul that—

> ✠ The sufferings of this present time are not worth comparing with the glory that is to be revealed to us. *Romans 8:18*

In Old Testament days God ordered His people to stop all work on the Sabbath. That day of rest was to remind them of the eternal rest they would someday have in heaven. Scripture shows that the Sabbath was to be a reminder of heaven when it says: "There remains a Sabbath rest for the people of God" (Hebrews 4:9). Thus also our Christian Sunday is to be a weekly reminder that Jesus arose from the grave on the first day of the week. It also reminds us of the peace and rest of heaven.

In the seventh chapter of Revelation God permits us, as it were, to put our hands on the window ledge of heaven and catch a quick glance. We see who is there: those who "have washed their robes and made them white in the blood of the Lamb." We see what they are doing: they "serve Him [God] day and night." We see how God cares for them: "He who sits upon the throne will shelter them with His presence." There we find Jesus, too. "The Lamb in the midst of the throne will be their Shepherd, and He will guide them to springs of living water." All suffering, now past, has given way to the peace of God's people. "They shall hunger no more, neither thirst anymore"; "God will wipe away every tear from their eyes."

THE CHRISTIAN BELIEVES: Jesus Will Give Me Everlasting Life

I know that I do not deserve God's wonderful gift of life. Sin closes the door of heaven in my face. With His forgiveness my Savior opens it again. Confidently I look forward to eternal life.

At the same time I do not despise the world in which God has placed me. He wants me to be His witness in this world. I take care not to become too attached to it or anything in it. The world is not my permanent home. In it I am a stranger and a pilgrim. Someday I must leave it. That will be no loss for me, for then I will be on the way to my real home.

When I die, God will take me to Himself. There in heaven I will live in perfect peace and joy forever. With the psalmist I raise my voice in gratitude to say:

Thou dost show me the path of life; in Thy presence there is fullness of joy, in Thy right hand are pleasures for evermore.   *Psalm 16:11*

Prayer Thought—

I thank God for preparing heaven for
His own. I thank Him that He has placed
me on the road to heaven by calling me
to faith in Jesus. I ask for His help that
I may bring to others the wonderful good
   news of life forever.

I'm but a stranger here, Heaven is my home;
Earth is a desert drear, Heaven is my home.
Danger and sorrow stand Round me on every hand;
Heaven is my fatherland, Heaven is my home.

Therefore I murmur not, Heaven is my home;
Whate'er my earthly lot, Heaven is my home;
And I shall surely stand There at my Lord's right hand.
Heaven is my fatherland, Heaven is my home.

Hymn 660, stanzas 1 and 4

177

"I cry with my voice to the Lord"
Psalm 142:1

Section IV: The Lord's Prayer

37. **Christian Prayer**
38. **Praying to Our Father**
39. **Hallow God's Name**
40. **May God's Kingdom Come**
41. **God's Will Be Done**
42. **Our Father and Our Daily Bread**
43. **Forgiven and Forgiving**
44. **The Christian's Help in Battle**
45. **Set Free from Evil's Power**
46. **It Shall Be So**

37

Christian Prayer

"Behold, he is praying." (Acts 9:11)
With these words the Lord announced that Saul of Tarsus had become a Christian. Saul had been a bitter foe of Jesus' followers. When Jesus appeared to Saul on the Damascus road, the Holy Spirit began to work in the heart of the Christ-hater. Later the Lord sent a believer named Ananias to speak with Saul. Ananias hesitated. The Lord reassured him that Saul was praying and that Saul would become a Christian missionary.

Being Christian and praying go hand in hand. As a hymn writer reminds us:

> Prayer is the Christian's vital breath,
> The Christian's native air.

We are about to get better acquainted with the prayer that God's people call the Lord's Prayer or the Our Father. It will mean more if we first think about the wonderful privilege of praying.

THIS IS THE CHRISTIAN FAITH: **In Christ We Have the Privilege of Speaking to Our God in Prayer**

Jesus suffered, died, and rose again to "save" all men. Those who believe in Him are saved. To be saved includes many blessings. We can sum it all up by saying that a believer is a child of God — in this world and forever.

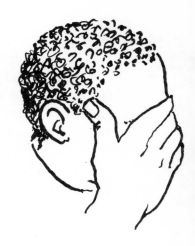

Since God is their Father, Christians want to talk to Him. God also wants His children to talk to Him.

The privilege of prayer flows from God's love. God commands His people to pray to Him. His command is really a gracious, gentle invitation. It is no harsh order when He says:

✠ Call upon Me in the day of trouble; I will deliver you, and you shall glorify Me.
Psalm 50:15

God shows His desire to hear His people's prayers when He promises to listen. There is no mistaking the promise in His offer, for He says:

✠ Ask, and it will be given you; seek, and you will find; knock, and it will be opened to you.
Matthew 7:7

In prayer Christians show what a blessing it is to have such a wonderful God. He is their Creator. He is their Redeemer. He is their Protector. He offers them eternal life.

God is worthy of their worship. This "worthship" of their God is a highly important matter for the Christian. The word "worthship" is related to the word "worship." And that is what worship is—telling God in respectful words how wonderful we think He is. Prayer is at the very heart of worship.

Men everywhere feel that belief in God and prayer go together. Even those who believe in false gods try to pray. The prophets of Baal cried all day to their god. Only Elijah, who prayed to the true God, received an answer. Prayer is answered only when directed to the living God. Jesus Himself rejected prayer to any but the true God, saying:

You shall worship the Lord your God, and Him only shall you serve.
Matthew 4:10

181

Christians emphasize that prayer must be made in Jesus' name. Only in Jesus do we have the right to pray, and in His intercession our prayer has power. On several occasions Jesus reminded His followers of this blessed privilege, for example:

If you ask anything of the Father, He will give it to you in My name.
John 16:23

How much do we pray? St. Paul says that we should never stop praying (1 Thessalonians 5:17). An unbeliever might exclaim: "A lifetime of prayer? What do you find to talk about?"

Ask a Christian, or study the prayers in the Bible. Sometimes Christians *adore* God. They *confess* their sins to Him daily. As they go through life, God showers them with blessings. For these they *thank* Him. As they need many things for body and soul, they *request* God's gifts in prayer.

In asking for physical blessings, Christians leave the outcome to their loving Father. They add "if it be Thy will" to their requests. In asking for spiritual blessings, they know that it is His will.

When they have finished praying for themselves, Christians have just begun to pray. They take also the needs of their fellowmen to God. Like Moses (Numbers 21:7), they have the right, the privilege, and the responsibility to pray for others. Hence they pray for their families. friends, and church and pastor. As good citizens they pray for their country and its leaders. They pray for those who are ill, in danger, or in need. They even pray for their enemies. Many Christians keep a written prayer list of people and things to pray for. In this way they truly act as "priests of the Lord."

182

St. Paul urged that Christians carry out a "ministry of prayer" when he wrote:

✠ I urge that supplications, prayers, intercessions, and thanksgivings be made for all men, for kings and all who are in high positions.

1 Timothy 2:1-2a

Christians are confident in prayer. They pray humbly, sincerely, often, and in Jesus' name.

THE CHRISTIAN BELIEVES: I May Truly Pray to God in Jesus' Name

As a Christian I am a "king and priest" before God. Prayer is an important part of my life as God's child.

I am tempted to neglect prayer. It is easy to pray without thinking or to forget to pray. I forget to pray for others; I am tempted to repeat words and not really work as I pray.

Repentantly I join the psalmist and cry:

✠ Let the words of my mouth and the meditation of my heart be acceptable in Thy sight, O Lord, my Rock and my Redeemer.

Psalm 19:14

Prayer Thought—

I thank God for the privilege of prayer.
I ask Him to answer my prayers for
Jesus' sake. I ask the Holy Spirit to make
my prayers worthy in God's sight.

Prayer is the soul's sincere desire,
Unuttered or exprest,
The motion of a hidden fire
That trembles in the breast.

Prayer is the simplest form of speech
That infant lips can try;
Prayer the sublimest strains that reach
The Majesty on high.

Prayer is the Christian's vital breath,
The Christian's native air,
His watchword at the gates of death—
He enters heaven with prayer.

Hymn 454, stanzas 1, 3, and 5

38

Praying to Our Father

"Lord, teach us to pray."

Jesus' disciples came to Him with that request one day. He did not make a long speech about prayer. He gave them an example to follow.

The people of God call that model prayer the Lord's Prayer. Some refer to it by the first two words of the prayer. They call it the Our Father.

Since the day when Jesus spoke the prayer it has been prayed daily in hundreds of languages by millions of God's people. It has been set to beautiful music. It has been carved into stone. It has been engraved in gold.

Jesus told His followers to begin prayer by saying the opening words of the *Lord's Prayer*.

Our Father who art in heaven.

What does this mean?

Here God encourages us to believe that He is truly our Father and we are His children. We therefore are to pray to Him with complete confidence just as children speak to their loving father.

THIS IS THE CHRISTIAN FAITH: We May Pray Confidently as to a Father

God is our Father in Christ.

That sentence is quickly said. However, we should not forget what had to be done to make this possible.

Behind that sentence is all the work of the triune God. To make it possible, God the Father showed His great mercy to a world of sinful people. He sent His Son to be the Sin-Bearer. To make it possible, Jesus became a human being. He suffered and died and rose again. To make it possible, the Holy Spirit worked in the Bible writers so that all might know about God's love. To make it possible, Christ founded the church to proclaim the Good News. By the preaching of God's Word and by Baptism the Holy Spirit continues to make sinful human beings the children of God. All that we remember at Christmas and Epiphany, on Good Friday, Easter, and Pentecost is involved when we say, "God is our Father in Christ."

St. Paul explains how all the work of God makes people God's children:

> ✠ For in Christ Jesus you are all sons of God through faith. For as many of you as were baptized into Christ have put on Christ.
>
> *Galatians 3:26-27*

Christians may not always appreciate the wonder that God accepts them as His children. False, man-made religions do not give this comfort. Such religions teach man that they are to be afraid of the gods. That is why St. Paul had to tell some people who had just come to faith in Jesus:

> For you did not receive the spirit of slavery to fall back into fear, but you have received the spirit of sonship. When we cry, "Abba! Father!" it is the Spirit Himself bearing witness with our spirit that we are children of God. *Romans 8:15-16*

When God invites His people to think of Him as their Father, He means that He is a kind and loving God. Not all earthly fathers are good. Some ignore their children. Some mistreat their children.   God

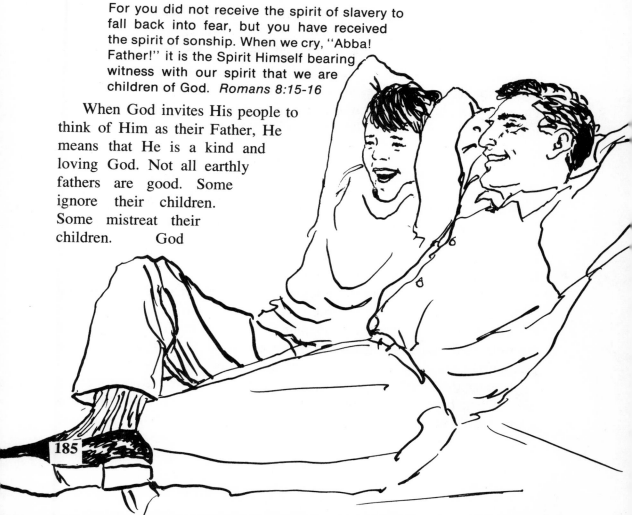

wants us to know that He is better than the best earthly father. Jesus made this comparison when He said:

> If you then, who are evil, know how to give good gifts to your children, how much more will your Father who is in heaven give good things to those who ask Him?   *Matthew 7:11*

Our God *can* promise to hear and answer the prayers of His people. Our Father is "in heaven." That means that He has the power to back up His promises. As the psalmist points out:

> Our God is in the heavens; He does whatever He pleases. *Psalm 115:3*

The invitation to pray comes from our God who is kind, loving, wise, and powerful. Therefore, God's people come to Him *with complete confidence.*

God's people do not wait to pray until they have tried everything else. They do not say: "Maybe it will do some good to pray. Let us try it." To pray in doubt is not praying as to a loving Father. St. James almost makes fun of people who pray without trusting God:

> Let him ask in faith, with no doubting, for he who doubts is like a wave of the sea that is driven and tossed by the wind.   *James 1:6*

Christians know that in their prayers they do not always ask for what is best for them. Nevertheless, they speak to the Lord as best they can. Then they are certain that God understands. He will in His great wisdom answer with what is best. They are ready to accept His answer.

THE CHRISTIAN BELIEVES: My Heavenly Father Hears My Prayers

If I have a good earthly father, I am grateful. Yet I am even more grateful to have a Father in heaven.

Many times I may feel like saying, "No one understands me. No one knows how I feel." This is not true. Even if every human being leaves me, there is my Father in heaven. I can pour out my heart to Him. He made me. He redeemed me. He forgives me. He accepts me. If I hesitate to use the privilege of prayer, I deny myself a great blessing.

I begin the Lord's Prayer by saying the word "Our." I do not come alone when I pray. As I pray, millions of my fellow Christians are also praying. I think of them. I pray with them and for them. Together we are

the church, the people of God. Remembering all that God has done for me and in me, I am ready to join the church in saying:

✠ Let us then with confidence draw near to the throne of grace, that we may receive mercy and find grace to help in time of need.

Hebrews 4:16

Prayer Thought—

I thank God for telling me that He is my Father. I confess my sins of neglect of prayer and ask forgiveness. I ask Him to make me a worthy child of God. I ask for the guidance of the Holy Spirit when I pray so that I may pray confidently.

Our Father, Thou in heaven above,
Who biddest us to dwell in love,
As brethren of one family,
To cry in every need to Thee,
Teach us no thoughtless words to say,
But from our inmost heart to pray.

Hymn 458, stanza 1

187

39

Hallow God's Name

What kind of reputation does God have?
God is perfect. Surely also His reputation should be perfect. Not so. A person's reputation is what other people think of him. Everyone *ought* to think that God is great and holy. Yet many people ignore God. Some even think of Him as foolish or evil.

God puts His own people on the spot. He reminds them that *they* are largely responsible for what others think of Him. A father gets part of the blame if his son is wicked. A school gets a bad name if its students misbehave. Even a whole country can get a bad name from a few rude citizens.

A believer's godly witness depends on God's work in his life. That is why this petition is so important. The *First Petition* asks God to do His work in us.

Hallowed be Thy name.

What does this mean?
God's name certainly is holy in itself, but we ask in this prayer that we may keep it holy.

When does this happen?
God's name is hallowed whenever His Word is taught in its truth and purity and we as children of God live in harmony with it. Help us to do this, heavenly Father!

THIS IS THE CHRISTIAN FAITH: God's People Hallow His Name by Pure Teaching and Holy Living

God's name is holy in itself. No one can make God more perfect. However, as the sun can be hidden by a cloud, so God's glory may be clouded from men's eyes.

God's people do not want to cloud out His glory. They pray to be kept from doing anything to make others think less of God. Their teachings and life influence the attitude of others toward God. Worldly people may say, "He's not much of a God if His people act bad and do not know what He says."

In his explanation of this petition, Dr. Luther seems to change the subject from God's name to God's Word. But properly understood, he does not. God's name is everything by which He makes Himself known. Especially in His Word does He reveal Himself. When by word and deed we use God's Word to His praise and honor, we make His name holy among us.

God's people believe that they honor God's name when they *rightly teach* what God has revealed in the Scriptures.

Christians must *not keep silent* about God's Word. No one can honor God unless God's people make His message known to the world. A witness is useful only when he correctly repeats what he has seen and heard. If he is silent, he is in a sense a liar. Jesus has appointed every one of His people as a witness for Him. Just before He ascended He said:

> ✠ You shall be My witnesses in Jerusalem and in all Judea and Samaria
> and to the end of the earth. *Acts 1:8b*

Christians must not *change* God's Word. People have a right to their own opinions in many things. But they have no right to teach their own ideas as God's truth. Of those who teach God's Word God says through Jeremiah:

> Let the prophet who has a dream tell the dream, but let him who has
> My Word speak My Word faithfully. *Jeremiah 23:28*

If God's people change God's Word or ignore parts of it, others will get wrong ideas about God. They might even miss the important message that God forgives sins for Jesus' sake.

Moreover, Christians ought always to live according to God's Word. Even when they fail, as they often do, they pray the more fervently for strength to follow His will. The First Petition really means: "God, help us to teach Your Word rightly and to live to please You."

It is not enough just to read the Bible, study it in confirmation class, and say one's prayers. The message of love to God and man must be lived all the time and everywhere.

The people of the world will judge God by the actions of His people. God sets His people up as advertisements for Him. It may be uncomfortable to be considered an example, but we can't escape it. Jesus said:

> Let your light shine before men that they may see your good works and give glory to your Father who is in heaven.   *Matthew 5:16*

People of the world may merely read the Bible and never go to church, but they cannot help seeing God's people every day. In a way, they read God's people. That's exactly what God intends. St. Paul put it that way:

> You are a letter from Christ delivered by us, written not with ink but with the Spirit of the living God, not on tablets of stone but on tablets of human hearts.   *2 Corinthians 3:3*

God's people pray: "Help us to be letters that glorify God."

THE CHRISTIAN BELIEVES: God Will Help Me
Hallow His Name

I cannot hide in the crowd and think it doesn't matter whether or not I teach or live according to God's Word.

Often I will be the only believer present to stand up for God. How will I glorify God? Will I pretend I don't know what God teaches? Will I agree with false teaching to avoid an argument? Will I try to remain popular by breaking God's law? Or will I live as if God's reputation depends upon me?

Left to myself, I cannot hallow God's name. I am too weak. Never will I pray, "Hallowed be Thy name," as if it were easy. For me it will ever be a cry for God to make me strong for His glory.

190

Prayer Thought—

I will first confess that at
times I have brought dishonor
to God by my life. Accepting
His forgiveness, I will pray
for strength and courage to
teach God's Word rightly and
to live that He may be
honored by all who know me.

Thy name be hallowed. Help us, Lord,
In purity to keep Thy Word,
That to the glory of Thy name
We walk before Thee free from blame.
Let no false doctrine us pervert;
All poor, deluded souls convert.

Hymn 458, stanza 2

TELEPHONE

191

40

May God's Kingdom Come

Kings are rare people in the modern world. Changes in governments have done away with much of the glory of crown and throne.

Christians persist in calling their God "King." In the Holy Scriptures God frequently calls Himself "King." To God's people the words "kingdom of God" are rich with meaning. It is fitting that in the Lord's Prayer Jesus reminds His followers to pray for the gracious ruling of God in their own hearts and lives as we do in the *Second Petition*.

Thy kingdom come.

What does this mean?
God's kingdom comes indeed without our praying for it, but we ask in this prayer that it may come also to us.

When does this happen?
God's kingdom comes when our heavenly Father gives us His Holy Spirit, so that by His grace we believe His holy Word and live a godly life on earth now and in heaven forever.

THIS IS THE CHRISTIAN FAITH: God's Kingdom Comes as the Holy Spirit Works Faith in Human Hearts

Jesus often spoke of His kingdom. Many of His parables begin, "The kingdom of heaven is like. . . ." He compared it to a large plant (tree), growing from a small seed. He said it spreads as yeast goes through all the bread dough. He pictured people being invited into the Kingdom as a king invites people to the prince's wedding party. Even the humblest people come to know that Jesus' kingdom is for all who accept Him as their Lord.

Jesus also spoke directly about the Kingdom. He began His teaching in Galilee by announcing:

> ✠ The time is fulfilled, and the kingdom of God is at hand; repent, and believe in the Gospel. *Mark 1:15*

Our Lord emphasized that He had not come to set up an earthly kingdom. This disappointed many people who hoped He had come to lead armies against the Roman Empire. Before Pilate Jesus agreed that He was a king. He explained, however, that His kingdom was "not of this world." (John 18:36)

St. Paul's advice to some people who tried to make the kingdom of God a matter of rules about food helps us to understand the Kingdom.

> ✠ For the kingdom of God does not mean food and drink but righteousness and peace and joy in the Holy Spirit. *Romans 14:17*

What, then, *is* the kingdom of God for which Christians pray? The words of Jesus and St. Paul explain that it is the rule of God over people who repent of their sins. It is present where people believe in the Gospel of God's love in Christ. It is present where the Holy Spirit is at work. It is present where people are righteous in God's sight because Jesus has paid the penalty for their sins. The kingdom of God is *both* God's ruling activity and the place or people where that ruling takes place.

The kingdom of God is Christ ruling in people's hearts. It begins here on earth as the Good News is told. It comes as lost sinners are rescued from Satan's grasp and placed among God's people. It keeps on coming as God's people share the Good News with others. It will finally come when God ends this world and rules among His people forever in heaven.

On earth God rules His people by offering His love. Such rule His people call "the kingdom of grace." In heaven God will reign in splendor.

193

His people call that "the kingdom of glory." The kingdom of grace is the church on earth. The kingdom of glory is the church in heaven.

The work of bringing people to faith is all God's. Therefore the Kingdom comes "of itself, without our prayer."

Yet Christians pray for it to come. This is, first, a prayer for themselves. By such prayer a Christian asks the Holy Spirit to work in his heart. "Turn me to Jesus and His cross," he prays. "Make me Your child."

But this petition is also a prayer for the mission work of the church. "Make your kingdom bigger, Lord. Bring more people into it." In so praying God's people also acknowledge that God has chosen them as witnesses to His Gospel. Included is the prayer that God would make each of us His missionary and that He would bless the work of all who tell the good news of Jesus' sacrifice. Christians are always eager to see God's family grow. The more brothers and sisters there are in the family of God, the happier they are. Christians heed the pleas of missionaries who cry with Paul:

> Brethren, pray for us, that the Word of the Lord may speed on and triumph, as it did among you.   *2 Thessalonians 3:1*

THE CHRISTIAN BELIEVES: I Pray and Work for God's Kingdom

I am grateful that the Holy Spirit has called me into God's kingdom of grace. I look forward confidently to entering the kingdom of glory.

Meanwhile I am concerned with the spread of the Kingdom. I will speak the Good News courageously and live a life that will draw others to Jesus. As one redeemed by Christ I will pray for the missionaries of the church and find ways to support them with my gifts. God has made me the church, too.

Prayer Thought—

I pray: Lord, feed my faith by Your Word that I may remain in the Kingdom forever. Make me care about the people who are not yet in Your kingdom. Make me bold to tell the good news about Jesus. Make me generous in my support of mission work.

Thy kingdom come. Thine let it be
In time and in eternity.
Let Thy good Spirit e'er be nigh
Our hearts with graces to supply.
Break Satan's power, defeat his rage;
Preserve Thy Church from age to age.

Hymn 458, stanza 3

195

41

God's Will Be Done

"The will of the Lord be done."
With these words, a group of people in Caesarea said good-bye to Paul and his company. Paul determined to go on to Jerusalem even though the prophet said he would be arrested there. His friends tried to persuade him not to go. But when Paul insisted that he was ready even to die for the Lord Jesus, they let him go. They prayed that God's will would prevail. (Acts 21:14)

God's will is best for His people. Sometimes His people cannot understand the wisdom of His will. Therefore Jesus taught us to pray in the *Third Petition* that God would carry out His will among us.

Thy will be done on earth as it is in heaven.

What does this mean?
The good and gracious will of God is surely done without our prayer, but we ask in this prayer that it may be done also among us.

When does this happen?
God's will is done when He hinders and defeats every evil scheme and purpose of the devil, the world, and our sinful self, which would prevent us from keeping His name holy and would oppose the coming of His kingdom. And His will is done when He strengthens our faith and keeps us firm in His Word as long as we live. This is His gracious and good will.

THIS IS THE CHRISTIAN FAITH: God's People Trust Him to Carry Out His Will for Them and in Them

God's will is more than a wish. It is His strong desire. He is ready to use His great power and wisdom and love to bring it about.

God's will plainly states that He wants all people to hallow His name and to be a part of His kingdom. God wants all people to be true believers.

St. Paul urges Christians to pray for all people because –

✠ God our Savior . . . desires all men to be saved and to come to the knowlege of the truth. *1 Timothy 2:4*

It is not only that God wants people to go to heaven someday. He wants them to be His people now. He wants them to be His witnesses now. He wants them to lead holy lives now. Christians are advised:

✠ Do not be conformed to this world but be transformed by the renewal of your mind, that you may prove what is the will of God, what is good and acceptable and perfect. *Romans 12:2*

God's will for His people sometimes includes suffering. At such times their faith upholds them. God's will is gracious and good. With trusting hearts they may pray as the Savior did:

✠ Father, if Thou art willing, remove this cup from Me; nevertheless not My will but Thine be done. *Luke 22:42*

If God's will were done on earth as it is in heaven, this earth would be a heaven. But there is still great need to pray that God's will may be done among men. There are strong counsels and wills that oppose God's will.

The *devil* opposes God's will. Right in the Garden of Eden he blocked God's plan for a perfect human race. But Jesus came to beat down the devil. His death on the cross meant Satan's defeat. Satan still works hard to make men miserable and turn them from God. Therefore God's people lean on God's promise:

✠ The Lord is faithful; He will strengthen you and guard you from evil. *2 Thessalonians 3:3*

The *world* opposes God's will. The world means all those who are not God's people by faith in Jesus. With cleverness they try to pull God's people into their way of life. It was the world at work when Herod beheaded John the Baptist to please Salome and her mother. But the Christian knows —

[Christ] gave Himself for our sins to deliver us from the present evil age. *Galatians 1:4*

Our own *flesh* opposes God's will. Even though we are God's children, we still have desires that are not wholly under the control of the Holy Spirit. Doubts, fears, and desires burn in us to make us forget God and turn to the devil's way. It was the flesh that drove Judas to betray Christ for a handful of silver coins.

198

God's will and the evil counsels are in a constant state of war. But victory for God is certain. God's will is done without our prayer. Many people have already been saved. Many more will reach the haven of eternal life. Yet, as long as a Christian is in this world, he is in danger. Without God man's doom is sealed. The enemy is too strong. In desperate need God's people take refuge in God. "Lord," they cry, "let *Your* will be done in us and for us."

THE CHRISTIAN BELIEVES: God's Will for Me Is My Guide and My Comfort

As God's child I will always seek to discover God's will for me. I know that His will is that I be His child now and forever. I will ask for the wisdom of the Holy Spirit that I may know, agree with, and follow His will day by day.

Throughout life I will be aware of the guiding hand of my God. Even in darkest days I will be comforted. God has called me to share in His kingdom. He controls my life.

By God's grace I am also a channel of God's gracious will. I can speak to others for God. I can heal and help others for God. Through me God can express His will for my fellowmen.

Prayer Thought —

> I ask God to show His will for my life
> day by day. I ask His protection against
> the will of the devil, the world, and my
> own flesh. I ask to be used by God as
> He works out His will for others.

> Thy gracious will on earth be done
> As 'tis in heaven before Thy throne;
> Obedience in our weal and woe
> And patience in all grief bestow.
> Curb flesh and blood and every ill
> That sets itself against Thy will.
>
> *Hymn 458, stanza 4*

42

Our Father and Our Daily Bread

How did bread get into the Lord's Prayer?
It seems natural to think of Bibles, folded hands, and hymns in connection with God. But how do you connect God and bread?

Jesus taught His disciples to pray for bread. God created the bodies of His people. He knows that the bodies need food and other things. Anything a child of God needs is a matter of concern to God. Therefore God's people are confident as they pray also for their earthly needs in the words of the *Fourth Petition*.

Give us this day our daily bread.

What does this mean?
God gives daily bread, even without our prayer, to all people, though sinful, but we ask in this prayer that He will help us to realize this and to receive our daily bread with thanks.

What is meant by "daily bread"?
Daily bread includes everything needed for this life, such as food and clothing, home and property, work and income, a devoted family, an orderly community, good government, favorable weather, peace and health, a good name, and true friends and neighbors.

THIS IS THE CHRISTIAN FAITH: God's People Receive Earthly Blessings from God with Thanksgiving

God provides for the needs of all His creatures. Even ungodly people enjoy His blessings. Whether they pray or not, people get a share of food and the other things they need for life. God's goodness is seen as —

> He makes His sun rise on the evil and on the good and sends rain on the just and on the unjust. *Matthew 5:45b*

God's people and the people of the world view their earthly belongings differently. The unbeliever often has great joy in things. And he feels that the things he has, he has gotten all by himself. He buys them; he makes them; he grows them; he gets them somehow. God warned His people against pride, saying:

> Beware lest you say in your heart, "My power and the might of my hand have gotten me this wealth." *Deuteronomy 8:17*

The rich farmer whom God called a fool did not recognize God as the Giver. He spoke of his possessions as *my* crops, *my* barns, *my* grain, *my* goods, and even *my* soul.

201

The child of God considers nothing solely his own. Humbly he admits that he is dependent upon his Father. This he confesses when he prays, "Father, give me." Of the world and its wonders he exclaims:

> ✠ O Lord, how manifold are *Thy* works! In wisdom hast *Thou* made them all. *Psalm 104:24*

God's people receive their earthly blessings from God. The blessings do not come directly from the sky as the manna and quail came to the Israelites. Our blessings do come from the same loving God, but He uses less direct ways of giving.

In asking God for earthly gifts, Christians carefully say, "Give us *our* bread." They desire only what God intends for *them*. To strongly want the things God plans for others is coveting.

However the word *our* shows concern for others. Christians consider it a privilege to give to others in the name of Christ. Christians have many projects by which they help those in need. Constantly they heed the apostle's reminder—

> Do not neglect to do good and to share what you have, for such sacrifices are pleasing to God. *Hebrews 13:16*

In looking to God for bodily needs Christians show that they trust the wisdom of God. They show this trust when they say "daily" and "this day." People of the world often think that everything depends upon themselves. Knowing no heavenly Father, they worry. The old fleshly nature of the Christian puts worry into his heart, too. As a child of God, however, he quiets his heart with the knowledge of his Savior's love. The same Jesus who fed a crowd with a boy's lunch says:

> Therefore do not be anxious, saying, "What shall we eat?" or "What shall we drink?" or "What shall we wear?" For the Gentiles seek all these things; and your heavenly Father knows that you need them all. But seek first His kingdom and His righteousness, and all these things shall be yours as well. *Matthew 6:31-33*

A Christian sees all His earthly gifts as coming from God's grace. With all the members of God's family he is—

> ✠ Always and for everything giving thanks in the name of our Lord Jesus Christ to God the Father. *Ephesians 5:20*

The first concern of God's people is the kingdom of God. God gives forgiveness in Christ and eternal life. Christians then discover that God gives them gifts also for their bodies.

THE CHRISTIAN BELIEVES: I Ask for and Use Bodily Blessings as God's Child

That I am a child of God will be evident as I attend worship services, pray, and study God's Word. My relation to God shows also what use I make of His earthly blessings.

I will show that I depend upon God by asking Him for what I need. I will be content with what He gives me. I will fight against worry. I will prove my trust in God by my confidence in His care for me. For all He gives me I will give thanks. I will consider it a privilege to share with many others the gifts God sends me.

These responses cannot come from my sinful heart. As a new person in Christ, however, I can think and act as God's child.

Prayer Thought—

I ask for a heart that trusts God's
goodness; for a grateful heart to thank
Him rightly; for a generous heart to share
my blessings.

Give us this day our daily bread
And let us all be clothed and fed.
From war and strife be our Defense,
From famine and from pestilence,
That we may live in godly peace,
Free from all care and avarice.

Hymn 458, stanza 5

43

Forgiven and Forgiving

Every person in the world is in debt to God. He is born that way.
To fail to live in love toward God and other people is sin. Every sin keeps
a human being in debt to God. One cannot just let God and other people
alone. No one has a right to say, "I mind my own business." God answers,
"To show love *is* your business."

A man who has debts which he cannot pay is in trouble. He is unable
to call upon the friendship of the one to whom he owes the debt. Fellowship is broken by the debt.

The *Fifth Petition* of the Lord's Prayer helps us with this problem.
How in the world can we pray to God when we are already in such debt
to Him because of our sins?

**And forgive us our trespasses, as we forgive those who
trespass against us.**

What does this mean?

We ask in this prayer that our Father in heaven would not
hold our sins against us and because of them refuse to
hear our prayer. And we pray that He would give us everything by grace, for we sin every day and deserve nothing
but punishment. So we on our part will heartily forgive
and gladly do good to those who sin against us.

THIS IS THE CHRISTIAN FAITH: Christians Accept and Imitate God's Forgiving Grace

In praying for forgiveness Christians admit their guilt in God's eyes. It is no pretense when they say, "We are not worthy of God's goodness." God demands perfection. God does not water down His demands for anyone. Furthermore, God sees and condemns even sins of thought. Christians know the sad answer when the psalmist asks:

✠ If Thou, O Lord, shouldst mark iniquities, Lord, who could stand?

Psalm 130:3

In praying for forgiveness Christians admit that they are not able to rid themselves of their guilt. There is no way they can pay their debt to God. People who do not truly know God's law think that they themselves can make things right with God. They feel that they can balance their evil with a few seemingly good deeds.

In praying for forgiveness God's people are asking a tremendous

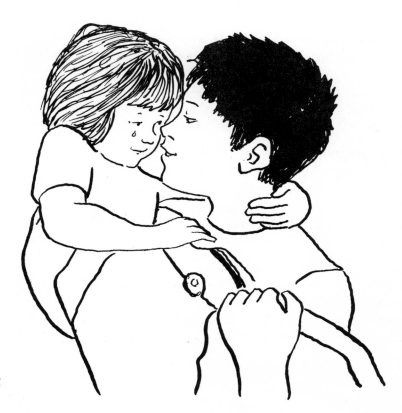

favor from God. It is not as if a poor man owed a rich man two dollars. He might say, "You will never miss two dollars among all your millions. Please do me this little favor." God is holy. He cannot dismiss any sin lightly. To forgive sins, God's own Son had to suffer and die. When we beg for forgiveness, we are asking God for the blessing of that terrible price. We are not asking God simply to turn His head and ignore our sins.

In praying for forgiveness, therefore, Christians show their faith. They are saying: "God, we are not worthy even to talk to You. Yet we believe that You will apply the price of Your own Son's death to our debts." Where does anyone get the boldness to make such a fantastic request? They get that faith from God Himself — through the Gospel.

What priceless gifts are God's people requesting in the Lord's Prayer? Look at the gift list: God, be our Father; God, make us live holy lives; God, take care of all our bodily needs; God, take us to life eternal. Why would anyone expect to receive such gifts? God's people believe that their heavenly Father is gracious. He offers all these things. He not only forgives their debt to Him; He also loads them with gifts beyond compare.

In praying for forgiveness God's people take on a duty. They want God to deal with them only in mercy. God agrees. Then He reminds them that they cannot change back from mercy to justice. They must deal in mercy with other people as God deals with them. Mercy travels from God to a man and from that man to his neighbor. Jesus said that it cannot work any other way:

> For if you forgive men their trespasses, your heavenly Father also will forgive you; but if you do not forgive men their trespasses, neither will your Father forgive your trespasses. *Matthew 6:14-15*

Christian forgiveness imitates God and not the world. People of the world in their forgiving others will often count and measure and bargain. Jesus showed the difference between worldly and divine mercy:

> Then Peter came up and said to Him, "Lord, how often shall my brother sin against me, and I forgive him? As many as seven times?" Jesus said to him, "I do not say to you seven times, but seventy times seven." *Matthew 18:21-22*

Christians reject the "eye for an eye" rule of the world. They believe that those whom they forgive are also entitled to loving help. Jesus said:

> "But I say to you that hear, love your enemies, do good to those who hate you, bless those who curse you, pray for those who abuse you." *Luke 6:27-28*

206

THE CHRISTIAN BELIEVES: My Forgiving Savior Expects Me to Forgive

The debt I cannot pay has been paid. God paid it for me at the cost of His Son's life. Through Him I am in fellowship with God.

God now asks me to pay a debt which I *can* pay in His power. He expects me to forgive those who hurt me. My wounded pride says, "Don't forgive." My flesh says, "Take revenge." My Savior says, "Forgive, My child, as I have forgiven you."

Prayer Thought—

> I humbly praise my Lord for granting me forgiveness at
> such a cost. I think of all who have injured me. I ask God
> to give me strength to forgive them and to show
> my love in practical ways.

Forgive our sins, Lord, we implore,
Remove from us their burden sore,
As we their trespasses forgive

Who by offenses us do grieve.
Thus let us dwell in charity
And serve our brother willingly.

Hymn 458, stanza 6

44

The Christian's Help in Battle

As long as they are in this world, Christians are in danger.
When the Holy Spirit brings a person to faith in Jesus, He is invading what was once the realm of the devil. The devil loses his claim on one of his subjects. The Christian becomes a member of the kingdom of God. New life is given to the believer. If nothing interferes, that new life will go on forever, beyond bodily death to eternity.

But the devil doesn't give up easily. He fights to keep people out of God's kingdom, and he battles to reclaim those whom he has lost. This is war. At stake are the souls of people. God wants them all, and the devil wants them all. From the creation of man in the Garden of Eden to the trumpet of the last Judgment the struggle rages.

The Christian realizes that he lives under the constant threat of losing his faith. Therefore he calls upon his Father to help. Jesus taught His disciples to pray for help, as we see in the next portion of the Lord's Prayer, the *Sixth Petition.*

And lead us not into temptation.

What does this mean?
God tempts no one to sin, but we ask in this prayer that God would watch over us and keep us so that the devil, the world, and our sinful self may not deceive us and draw us into false belief, despair, and other great and shameful sins. And we pray that even though we are so tempted we may still win the final victory.

THIS IS THE CHRISTIAN FAITH: God Keeps His Believers Safe in the Midst of Temptation

In any battle a person must know know his enemy. At first glance this petition seems to say that God Himself tries to get His people to fall away. But God has paid a great price to save His people. His desire is that they remain His disciples to all eternity. The petition does two things: it warns the Christian that he will be tempted, and it points him to God as his only refuge.

It is the devil, not God, who tempts Christians to sin and to doubt. The ungodly people of the world and the fleshly nature of the Christian are the devil's strong allies. Satan prefers to hide his purposes, but St. Peter unmasks the enemy:

> ✠ Be sober, be watchful. Your adversary the devil prowls around like a roaring lion, seeking someone to devour. *1 Peter 5:8*

The Bible shows God acting in mercy from the beginning of time. It also shows Satan working to destroy God's plan. Satan tempted Adam and Eve. He used Abraham's fear to get him to lie. Satan convinced both Moses and David to disobey God by counting the people of Israel in pride. He used hunger to get Esau to sell his birthright. He tempted Judas to betray Jesus and Peter to deny the Lord. He even attempted to draw Jesus away from His work of saving a lost world. The Bible records hundreds of ways by which Satan has fought against God and man.

There is a danger that God's people may underestimate the enemy. Satan is a fallen angel. He is wise and sly. He has unknown numbers of evil angels to do his work. No man by his own strength can withstand this force. Poverty or wealth, sickness or health, in fact anything may become a tool of Satan. When a Christian reaches a point in life where he must decide what to do, God and Satan point to opposite ways. God says, "This is the way to life." Satan says, "Go my way and really live." At the end of Satan's road is a cliff over which the sinner falls to destruction. St. Paul warns of the viciousness of the devil:

> ✠ For we are not contending against flesh and blood, but against the principalities, against the powers, against the world rulers of this present darkness, against the spiritual hosts of wickedness in the heavenly places. *Ephesians 6:12*

God helps the Christian in temptation by strengthening His people. Trials are then exercise to develop spiritual muscles. God says:

> Count it all joy, my brethren, when you meet various trials, for you know that the testing of your faith produces steadfastness. *James 1:2-3*

God also promises:

> ✠ God is faithful, and He will not let you be tempted beyond your strength, but with the temptation will also provide the way of escape, that you may be able to endure it. *1 Corinthians 10:13b*

God helps the Christian in temptation by halting the attacks of Satan in time. He reminds His people:

✠ The Lord knows how to rescue the godly from trial. *2 Peter 2:9a*

THE CHRISTIAN BELIEVES: God Gives Me Victory in Temptations

As a Christian I expect to be tempted by the devil, the world, and my flesh. I heed God's warnings and stay alert to danger. I do not gamble with my soul's safety by foolishly running into temptation.

I believe that Jesus defeated Satan and won my salvation. God keeps me by His Word. It is my sure defense, as the apostle writes:

✠ Therefore take the whole armor of God, that you may be able to withstand in the evil day.
                                                    Ephesians 6:13

Prayer Thought—

> I pray to be protected against the attacks of Satan. I ask God to be with me in trial. I pray that I may be wise, strong, and patient when I am tempted.

> Into temptation lead us not.
> When evil foes against us plot
> And vex our souls on every hand,
> Oh, give us strength that we may stand
> Firm in the faith, a well-armed host,
> Through comfort of the Holy Ghost!
>
> *Hymn 458, stanza 7*

211

45

Set Free from Evil's Power

Why would anyone call this world a "vale of tears"?
In many ways this is a happy world. God's people are not blind to the pleasures He gives for this life. Many Christians have a full measure of good things.

Yet there is much evil in the world. Accidents and death, sickness and sorrow, hatreds and wars, crime and poverty are everywhere. Furthermore, suffering and sorrow come to God's people as well as to the ungodly.

How does a Christian deal with the evil that comes into his life? As a child of God he turns in prayer to his heavenly Father. The Christian is traveling to heaven through an evil world. He puts his life in God's hands as he prays the last petition of the Lord's Prayer, the *Seventh.*

But deliver us from evil.

What does this mean?
We ask in this inclusive prayer that our heavenly Father would save us from every evil to body and soul, and at our last hour would mercifully take us from the troubles of this world to Himself in heaven.

THIS IS THE CHRISTIAN FAITH: God Frees His People from the Power of Evil

To a man who tries to live his life without God, evil is a terrible tyrant. Many an ungodly man counts on having this life only. Because he looks forward to nothing else, he feels cheated whenever anything unpleasant happens to him. He can be happy and content only when life is going his way. He protects himself from evil as best he can. But there are many forces which he cannot control. If something evil is not happening just now, at any moment some tragedy may come to make life bitter. Perhaps this explains why some people who seem to be well off commit suicide.

God's people do not enjoy suffering and sorrow. They do not look for trouble just to have it and bear it. They are grateful when their Father blesses them with a pleasant life. However, they believe that He can bless them also through evil happenings. In this petition of the Lord's Prayer

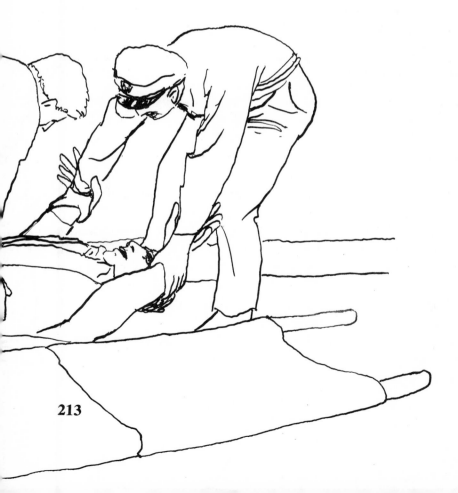

they do *not* pray, "Lord, don't ever let anything painful happen to us." God lets us know that He does permit suffering to come into the lives of His people. He uses suffering to strengthen Christians, as He says:

✠ It is for discipline that you have to endure. God is treating you as sons; for what son is there whom his father does not discipline?
Hebrews 12:7

The Christian believes that this life is just the beginning of his eternal life with God. A child of God is only passing through this world to a far better one. In this world, the devil and his helpers bring about as much evil as they can. Therefore God has given notice that—

✠ . . . through many tribulations we must enter the kingdom of God.
Acts 14:22b

The knowledge that God is working to bring them to heaven lifts Christians above the wicked world. They suffer pain, but they see through the darkness to the eternal glory. In spite of many troubles St. Paul could say:

So we do not lose heart. . . . For this slight momentary affliction is preparing for us an eternal weight of glory beyond all comparison, because we look not to the things that are seen but to the things that are unseen; for the things that are seen are transient, but the things that are unseen are eternal. *2 Corinthians 4:16-18*

In this petition God's people are not praying to *escape* evil. They are praying to be *set free* from the power of evil when it happens to them. They ask God to keep evil away from them if it is His will. But they especially ask that evil may not bind them in self-pity and bitterness. They ask that even in pain and sorrow they may still look to God in faith and hope. They desire to be brave and useful members of God's kingdom, no matter how suffering may attack them.

The heroes of the Christian church have been men and women whose voice of witness no suffering or trouble could stop. Even threats of death by torture could not keep Jesus' apostles from their work for God. Martin Luther created much trouble for himself when he insisted upon teaching the truth of God from the Holy Scriptures. Not all the power on earth could still his pen or silence his preaching.

Looking to the end of life on this earth, God's people ask to be taken to heaven. In praying for a blessed end they are not asking that they may die quietly. It is a blessing to die quietly, surrounded by loved ones.

But any death, no matter how violent, is blessed if it is the doorway to eternal life. Christians do not ask to be taken to heaven because of their own goodness. They believe that heaven is the gift of God to all who accept Jesus as their Savior. By means of death God plucks His Christians out of the reach of all evil. Free at last from sin and sufferings, the Christian will understand what God meant when He said through His apostle:

✠ Blessed is the man who endures trial, for when he has stood the test he will receive the crown of life which God has promised to those who love Him.

James 1:12

THE CHRISTIAN BELIEVES: My God Will Deliver Me from Evil's Power in This Life and Forever

I trust my God, for Jesus' sake, to protect me from every evil of body and soul, property and honor.

When evil comes to me, I believe that my God controls it. It cannot destroy my faith. It cannot make me lose my position as a child of God. And when I die, my God will take me into His everlasting kingdom.

Prayer Thought—

> I ask God to keep evil away from me,
> according to His will. I pray that the Lord
> will strengthen me to bear suffering
> cheerfully. I ask that I may be a useful
> member of God's kingdom in spite of any
> evil which may happen to me.

> From evil, Lord, deliver us;
> The times and days are perilous.
> Redeem us from eternal death,
> And when we yield our dying breath,
> Console us, grant us calm release,
> And take our souls to Thee in peace.

Hymn 458, stanza 8

46

It Shall Be So

Quite likely Jesus Himself did not speak the closing words of the Lord's Prayer. For this reason some Christians do not add them to the prayer.

However, worshipers in ancient times had the custom of adding a few words of praise to their prayers. Very early in the history of the church such a conclusion was added to the Lord's Prayer. We call it the

doxology. Men who copied the Bible wrote the words into their copies of Jesus' words in Matthew, chapter 6. The words were perhaps borrowed from the prayer of David in 1 Chronicles 29:11.

In the Lord's Prayer God's people ask for gifts which no man can give. An unbeliever might ask, "How do you expect to get an answer to such a bold prayer?" The church responds with a firm statement of faith in God, the *Conclusion* of the Lord's Prayer.

For Thine is the kingdom and the power and the glory forever and ever. Amen.

What does "Amen" mean?

Amen means *Yes, it shall be so*. We say *Amen* because we are certain that such petitions are pleasing to our Father in heaven and are heard by Him. For He Himself has commanded us to pray in this way and has promised to hear us.

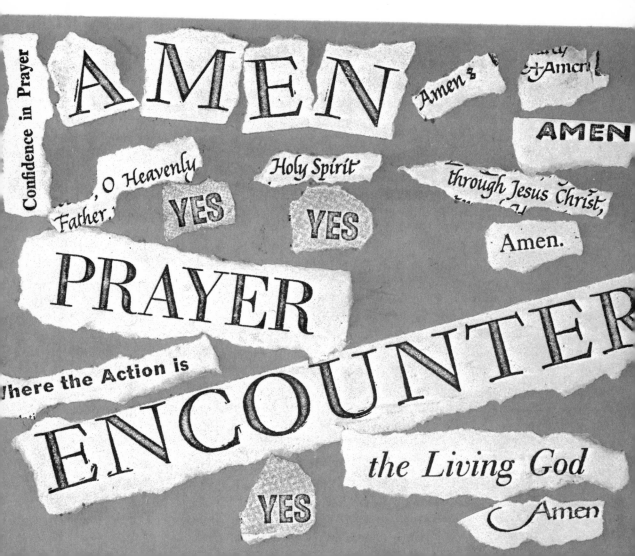

THIS IS THE CHRISTIAN FAITH: God's Kingship, Power, and Glory Give Power to Christian Prayer

When Christians pray, they are not just wishing or hoping. They are confident that God hears and responds to the prayers of His people.

Christians are confident in prayer because they believe that their God is King of the universe. To get something done it is best to ask the person who is in charge. In a family, parents are in charge. In a school, the teachers are in charge. In the universe, God is in charge. God's ruling is often hidden from human eyes. In ignorance men may think they are in charge. Or some people think that things happen only by chance. That means that no person is in charge of the universe. The Christian names his God as the One in charge of all this and says:

> ✠ Let them know that Thou alone, whose name is the Lord, art the Most High over all the earth. *Psalm 83:18*

Christians are confident in prayer because they believe that God is all-powerful. Furthermore, He is ready to use that power for them. It is useless to ask anyone for help unless he has the ability to help. The triune God has endless power available for His people. They rejoice to confess that—

> ✠ Both riches and honor come from Thee, and Thou rulest over all. In Thy hand are power and might; and in Thy hand it is to make great and to give strength to all. *1 Chronicles 29:12*

Christians are confident in prayer because they believe that God has the "glory." This means much more than that God's people thank Him for His gifts. It is more than just honor and fame. God's glory is His very *Presence*. Jesus is the glory of God, God present with men, as John wrote:

> We have beheld His glory, glory as of the only Son from the Father. *John 1:14b*

Jesus taught us this prayer. Jesus is the Presence of God and He assures us that the almighty God is our heavenly Father.

Jesus makes it possible for believers to take this prayer on their lips. God is our Father because Jesus died for us. Jesus came to keep God's name holy by His obedience. By His work as Redeemer the kingdom of God has come. He enables God's people to do God's will on earth. He Himself did His Father's will perfectly. He is the Good Shepherd who feeds the souls and bodies of His believers. By paying the price for the forgiveness of sins He defeated the power of sin and Satan for us. And at last He will welcome us into heaven—beyond all evil.

All this leads the Christian to say "Amen" at the end of this and other prayers. The word *Amen* is a Hebrew word. It means, "This is certain." It expresses the Christian faith that God hears and answers the prayers of His people.

Because they are confident, Christians pray often. They pray with their fellow Christians, and they pray alone. They pray for themselves, and they pray for others. They pray for spiritual blessings and bodily blessings. God Himself has done all that is needed to give prayer its power. In answer to His gracious call Christians urge one another:

✠ Let us then with confidence draw near to the throne of grace that we may receive mercy and find grace to help in time of need.

Hebrews 4:16

THE CHRISTIAN BELIEVES: God Almighty Gives Me the Privilege of Prayer

Prayer should not be a once-in-a-while activity for me. Nor should I let it be a mere mumbling of memorized words.

The Lord of the universe sacrificed His Son to give me the right to pray as His child. He commands me to pray and promises to answer. There is no reason for me to be meek or doubtful in prayer; I may storm the gates of heaven with my prayers. In Jesus' name I firmly say, "Amen! It shall be so!"

Prayer Thought—

> I thank God for all He has done to give me the privilege of prayer. I ask Him to make me bold to pray and thankful for His answers.

> Amen, that is, So shall it be.
> Confirm our faith and hope in Thee
> That we may doubt not, but believe
> What here we ask we shall receive.
> Thus in Thy name and at Thy word
> We say: Amen. Oh, hear us, Lord!

Hymn 458, stanza 9

"I am not ashamed of the Gospel; it is the power of God for salvation"
Romans 1:16

Section V: Word and Sacraments

47. God's Means of Grace
48. What Is Baptism?
49. Baptism's Blessings and Power
50. Baptism in Our Daily Lives
51. What Is the Sacrament of the Altar?
52. The Blessings and Power of the Lord's Supper
53. Getting Ready for the Sacrament
54. Claiming God's Promises
55. Ambassadors for Christ
56. The Special Ministry
57. Mutual Care and Discipline
58. Confession and Absolution

47

God's Means of Grace

Four words kept a boy alive. They were more than magic words. They brought God's love and power to him in his illness.

The sick boy was the son of a city official in Capernaum. His father learned that Jesus was in a nearby town. He knew Jesus had power to help his son. But how could he get Jesus' power to his son? He simply begged Jesus to come and help. Jesus answered the plea. He connected His power to the boy by speaking four words: "Your son will live." The man believed in Jesus. Before the father reached home, servants met him with the good news that the boy was well.

Jesus, the Son of God, stood behind those words. The same words spoken by someone else would have been useless. Because *Jesus* spoke the words, the boy was healed.

Just as Jesus used these four words to keep a boy alive, so God uses means to bring life to men today. God uses the words of the Holy Scriptures to call men to repentance and forgiveness. God uses ordinary water and His Word to make a sinner His child. God uses bread and wine and the Word to give forgiveness and life.

These are the Gospel and the sacraments. We call them the means of grace.

THIS IS THE CHRISTIAN FAITH: Through the Gospel and the Sacraments God Brings the Benefits of His Saving Work to His People

"I believe that I cannot by my own reason or strength believe in Jesus Christ, my Lord, or come to Him; but the Holy Ghost has called me by the Gospel." With these words Martin Luther begins his explanation of the work of God's Holy Spirit. God's Spirit alone can create faith in the heart of the sinner. By the power of God the sinner receives the blessings of forgiveness and life. The Spirit works through the Gospel.

Why doesn't everyone believe the promises of God? Human beings are by nature in Satan's power. They are blind to the things of God. They can see only this present world. Yet some come to faith in God. Where does this faith come from? St. Paul answers:

> ✠ So faith comes from what is heard, and what is heard comes by the preaching of Christ.
> *Romans 10:17*

When Lazarus was dead, Jesus stood at the grave and said, "Lazarus, come out." The words carried the power of God. Life flowed into the body of Lazarus. To bring spiritual life to people who are dead, God sends life through His Word. St. Peter writes of the life-giving power of God's Word:

> ✠ You have been born anew, not of perishable seed but of imperishable, through the living and abiding Word of God.
> *1 Peter 1:23*

223

To avoid any mistake about what he means by "Word of God," Peter adds:

✠ . . . but the Word of the Lord abides forever. That Word is the *good news* which was preached to you.   *1 Peter 1:25*

The means through which God works in men is the Word. Word thus means God at work. This Word of God judges the sinner. It shows him how helpless he is. This Word of God is the Law which drives sinners to the cross of Christ.

God's Word also calls men and brings them to life in Christ. This Word of God is the Gospel. It is the good news of God's gracious work for us in Jesus Christ. This good news can be in the spoken Word, the printed Word, or the message of a picture or other art production.

Beyond this, God has two special ways to bring forgiveness, life, and salvation to us. We call these the *sacraments*. There are two: Baptism and the Lord's Supper.

A sacrament is a sacred action. There are many sacred actions, such as kneeling or making the sign of the cross. Such actions help people as they worship. Sacraments are *different* because the Lord Himself instituted them and asks His people to use them. In each sacrament Christians use something which can be seen and touched. We call these "the external elements." In Baptism it is water. In the Lord's Supper it is bread and wine.

The most important thing to know about the sacraments is what *the Lord does* in them through His Word. The Holy Spirit works in the sacraments. In Baptism and the Lord's Supper God brings people the forgiveness of sins and power to live His life. God is in action in the sacraments as He is in the written witness of the Holy Scriptures.

THE CHRISTIAN BELIEVES: God Blesses Me Through His Word and Sacraments

God is so great. Sometimes He seems too far away. How can He reach me? How can He forgive my sins and change my heart?

There is God's Word close to me. There is my Bible; there is my Christian teacher; there is my pastor. Through my ears and eyes and brain God reaches me with His Word. Moreover, He has reached me with His Sacrament of Baptism. He offers me also the Lord's Supper. Through the sacraments God gives and seals His forgiveness and life to me. Through them He gives or strengthens my faith and makes me sure that I belong to Him. Through these means of grace He works in my heart and life.

Prayer Thought—

I thank God for preparing His Word and the sacraments by which He makes and keeps me as His own. I ask for wisdom to use these gifts faithfully.

And for this our soul's salvation
Voucheth Thy good Spirit, Lord,
In Thy Sacraments and Word.

He imparteth consolation,
Granteth us the gift of faith
That we fear nor hell nor death.

Hymn 384, stanza 3

48

What Is Baptism?

Suppose you want to tell the life story of a famous person. You can't tell the whole story at once. You list the events which directed his life and build the story around high points. Birth, schooling, marriage, becoming a parent, and getting a job are all important events.

In the life story of a Christian, Baptism is a high point. The Christian's entire life in this world and in the next gets a new direction from Baptism. That's why the Christian is eager to know more about this event. Martin Luther begins his explanation of the *Sacrament of Holy Baptism* in the following paragraphs:

> **What is Baptism?**
> Baptism is not water only, but it is water used together with God's Word and by His command.
> **What is this word?**
> In Matthew 28 our Lord Jesus Christ says: "Go therefore and make disciples of all nations, baptizing them in the name of the Father and of the Son and of the Holy Spirit."

THIS IS THE CHRISTIAN FAITH: **Baptism Is God's Way of Accepting People into His Kingdom**

What we can see in Baptism is simple. Someone puts water on a person being baptized and says, "I baptize you in the name of the Father and of the Son and of the Holy Ghost." Usually a pastor performs the ceremony, but any Christian may do it. The manner in which the water is applied is not important. It may be poured or sprinkled, or the person may be

immersed in a river or a tank. Appropriate Scripture readings and prayers are added to the ceremony, but they are not essential. In the case of infants, witnesses or sponsors may be chosen. The latter also promise to help the parents teach and guide the child.

The water of Baptism is connected with God's command and promise. His command is known as the Great Commission. St. Matthew recorded the words:

> ✠ And Jesus came and said to them, "All authority in heaven and on earth has been given to Me. Go therefore and make disciples of all nations, baptizing them in the name of the Father and of the Son and of the Holy Spirit, teaching them to observe all that I have commanded you; and lo, I am with you always, to the close of the age."
> *Matthew 28:18-20*

Our Lord commanded Baptism because He uses it for His purposes. In Baptism the living Lord reaches out to sinners. By it He works directly in each individual person.

In Baptism the living Lord creates a new relationship with a person. By birth we become children of our parents. By Baptism we become children of God. By Baptism God puts His brand upon us and claims us as His own. We are baptized "in the name of the Father and of the Son and of the Holy Ghost." That means that we get the benefit of all that the triune God has done for men. As God's children we receive His love and mercy and eternal life. As sinners we can claim no part in anything that is God's. After Baptism he who was a stranger becomes part of God's family. St. Paul describes the new relationship:

> ✠ So then you are no longer strangers and sojourners, but you are fellow citizens with the saints and members of the household of God.
> *Ephesians 2:19*

In Baptism the living Lord creates a new person. That is why the Lord speaks of it as a "new birth." To Nicodemus He explained:

> ✠ Truly, truly, I say to you, unless one is born of water and the Spirit, he cannot enter the kingdom of God. That which is born of the flesh is flesh and that which is born of the Spirit is spirit.   *John 3:5-6*

By natural birth we are enemies of God. By Baptism a whole new person comes into being. St. Paul is an example of this. Through Baptism Saul the persecutor became the apostle. He was so amazed by what happened to him that he called himself and other Christians "a new creation." (2 Corinthians 5:17)

In Baptism the living Lord initiates people into His kingdom. He then rules the life of the baptized Christian. Baptism is called "the sacrament of initiation." The baptized person becomes a full member of the church of Jesus Christ. He moves out of the power of Satan and becomes part of the body of Christ. The Bible says:

> ✠ He has delivered us from the dominion of darkness and transferred us to the kingdom of His beloved Son, in whom we have redemption, the forgiveness of sins. *Colossians 1:13-14*

All of this is God's doing. No one can do these things for himself. God can do these things for anyone—even tiny babies. Children are part of "all nations," whom God wants as disciples. They are born in sin and need to be transferred into Christ's kingdom. By Baptism the Holy Spirit does God's work in human hearts.

THE CHRISTIAN BELIEVES: My Baptism Makes Me a Child of God

As a baptized Christian I belong to God. Sin still works in me, but the Holy Spirit lives in my heart now. I am a member of God's kingdom. I am able to "live under Him in His kingdom" because in Baptism He gave me a new birth and a new life. My baptism is the most important event of my life. By it I have been directed toward eternal life with God.

Prayer Thought—

> I ask God to keep me aware that I am His child. I seek His strength that I may live under Him as a happy and useful member of His church.

> Baptized into Thy name most holy,
> O Father, Son, and Holy Ghost,
> I claim a place, though weak and lowly,
> Among Thy seed, Thy chosen host.
> Buried with Christ and dead to sin,
> Thy Spirit now shall live within.
>
> *Hymn 298, stanza 1*

229

49

Baptism's Blessings and Power

God sometimes wraps large gifts in small packages Who would have looked for a great king in the person of a shepherd named David? Or who would have expected to find the Son of God in a manger? Our God is a God of surprises,

What would anyone expect from a little water poured on his head? Knowing God's ways, we do not despise the humble act of baptism. Like children unwrapping a gift from a rich and kind father, God's people have discovered the blessings and power of Baptism. Dr. Luther tells about this in the following paragraphs.

What benefits does God give in Baptism?
In Baptism God forgives sin, delivers from death and the devil, and gives everlasting salvation to all who believe what He has promised.

What is God's promise?

In Mark 16 our Lord Jesus Christ says: "He who believes and is baptized will be saved; but he who does not believe will be condemned."

How can water do such great things?

It is not water that does these things, but God's Word with the water and our trust in this Word. Water by itself is only water, but with the Word of God it is a life-giving water which by grace gives the new birth through the Holy Spirit. St. Paul writes in Titus 3: "He saved us . . . in virtue of His own mercy, by the washing of regeneration and renewal in the Holy Spirit, which He poured out upon us richly through Jesus Christ our Savior, so that we might be justified by His grace and become heirs in hope of eternal life. The saying is sure."

THIS IS THE CHRISTIAN FAITH: Through His Word in Baptism, God Gives Great Blessings to Believers

Christians believe that God works forgiveness of sins through Baptism. God forgives sins only because Jesus paid the penalty for all men's sins. Baptism is not a payment which men make to God. It is God's way of bringing to people the forgiveness earned by Jesus. Baptism works everyday to keep on applying these benefits to the Christian. We might compare it somewhat to a smallpox vaccination. A vaccination once received goes on working against the disease for years. St. Peter leaves no doubt about Baptism's power to forgive sin, for he says:

✠ "Repent, and be baptized every one of you in the name of Jesus Christ for the forgiveness of your sins."   *Acts 2:38a*

Christians believe that through Baptism God delivers from death. Baptized people die. To be delivered from death means to go through death and be unhurt by it. Sinners deserve eternal death for disobeying

God. However, God accepts Jesus' death in their place. Baptism connects Christians with that death of Jesus, as St. Paul says:

✠ Do you not know that all of us who have been baptized into Christ Jesus were baptized into His death? *Romans 6:3*

Death lies *behind* the Christian. Baptism makes him alive to God. Bodily death will be only a portal to the never-ending life.

Christians believe that through Baptism God delivers from the devil. The devil is always striving to undo God's work. Satan fights in cunning ways to keep people out of God's kingdom. He argues and fights against every step a man takes toward God. Yet, we are not helpless before him. Jesus is our Champion. Says Luther, "But for us fights the Valiant One, whom God Himself elected." At the time of Baptism a Christian turns his back on Satan. He renounces the devil and all his wicked ways and works. No man can turn from Satan by human power. Jesus defeated Satan to make it possible, as the holy writer points out:

✠ Since therefore the children share in flesh and blood, He Himself likewise partook of the same nature, that through death He might destroy him who has the power of death, that is, the devil. *Hebrews 2:14*

Christians believe that through Baptism God gives eternal salvation. Salvation includes living in this life as one of God's people and then living with Him forever. It means to be rescued from living as if there were no God or heaven. In Baptism God places a person among the "company of the saved." It is the act by which God clothes His people with the garment of holiness that only Jesus has by nature, as St. Paul says:

✠ For as many of you as were baptized into Christ have put on Christ. *Galatians 3:27*

How can such a simple action as applying water do all this? We might ask how a piece of paper can give a man his daily food. Paper has little worth, but if it is a dollar bill, it has the promise of a strong government behind it. When citizens trust that promise, they use the paper money freely and get the benefits it brings. It isn't "just paper."

Baptism isn't "just water." It is water which carries the promise of God. Behind it stands the Creator of the world. Behind it stands the love God has shown in giving His Son as Savior. God uses Baptism to bring His power and love to bear upon people. How wise and good of God to arrange such a simple way of reaching sinful people!

Baptism is not a magic ritual. God gives the blessings to those who believe His promises. No man can add to Baptism's gifts. God does it all. God even works in us the ability to believe and accept His promises. It isn't that we go out to meet God halfway. God comes all the way to the sinner. We have the terrible power to refuse God's gifts. Yet, even in the offering of His gifts God enables us to accept them.

THE CHRISTIAN BELIEVES: God Blesses Me Every Day Through My Baptism

God made me His child. Baptism is an important part of that act. Because I am baptized, I am receiving the benefits my Savior earned for me and all men: my sins are forgiven; I am delivered from death; I am delivered from Satan's power; eternal salvation is mine. My baptism includes that I am adopted by God and have a right to all He offers.

Prayer Thought—

> I ask God to help me appreciate my
> baptism and rejoice in it. I am so blessed
> while so many others do not have this
> treasure. I pray for strength to work and
> speak and give that others may find the
> joy I have.

> He that believes and is baptized
> Shall see the Lord's salvation;
> Baptized into the death of Christ,
> He is a new creation.
> Through Christ's redemption he shall stand
> Among the glorious heavenly band
> Of every tribe and nation.
>
> *Hymn 301, stanza 1*

50

Baptism in Our Daily Lives

As we put water on our bodies to wash them, so Baptism signifies the cleansing of our lives from the stains of sin.

St. Paul saw another event in Baptism. It pictures a person being drowned. The water closes over him and he dies. But in Baptism God makes the new man rise. Dr. Luther used the following Biblical reference to explain this daily repentance and renewal in the life of the baptized child of God.

What does Baptism mean for daily living?
It means that our sinful self, with all its evil deeds and desires, should be drowned through daily repentance; and that day after day a new self should arise to live with God in righteousness and purity forever.

St. Paul writes in Romans 6: "We were buried therefore with Him by Baptism into death, so that as Christ was raised from the dead by the glory of the Father, we too might walk in newness of life."

THIS IS THE CHRISTIAN FAITH: Baptism Includes a Life of Repentance, Faith, and Godly Living

Baptism includes a daily dying for the Christian. That sounds strange. How can a person die every day and yet go on living? God's Word tells us that a Christian has two natures. The one "self" is the sinful person who begins to exist when a person is born. In the Christian, however, there is another "self." This is the new nature which God creates in Baptism. Within every Christian these two natures live together. The evil nature is called "old Adam." The new nature is called "new man."

The old Adam must be put to death every day. The old Adam works for Satan. Every day the Christian must fight this old Adam. At his baptism the Christian renounces the devil and his wicked works. Remembering his baptism means that the Christian renounces his own wicked desires. God says:

> Put off your old nature which belongs to your former manner of life and is corrupt through deceitful lusts. *Ephesians 4:22*

Baptism includes a daily renewing for the Christian. It is the daily concern of the Christian to let the "new man" rule him. As God's child, the Christian struggles to kill his evil nature. Therefore St. Paul continues:

> And be renewed in the spirit of your minds, and put on the new nature, created after the likeness of God in true righteousness and holiness. *Ephesians 4:23-24*

Baptism includes daily repentance for the Christian. Every Christian is a battlefield in a bitter war. It is the war between the old Adam and the new man. St. Paul complains about this bitter battle in these words:

> For I know that nothing good dwells within me, that is, in my flesh. I can will what is right, but I cannot do it. For I do not do the good I want, but the evil I do not want is what I do. . . . Wretched man that I am! *Romans 7:18-19, 24a*

The Christian echoes this lament. God's law shows him how his sinful nature has built the wall between himself and God. He sees how helpless he is to climb this wall or to tear it down. He confesses his sin to God; He dies to himself; He repents. This happens every day.

Baptism includes a daily acceptance of God's grace. In Baptism God says, "My Son died for you, so I accept you as My child." God stands by

235

that agreement forever. At baptism the Christian says, "I accept Your gift." Every day of his life the Christian confesses again, "I believe God's promise." Sometimes he confesses it quietly to God. Sometimes he confesses it so that others too may believe. Sometimes, as at confirmation, he confesses it solemnly before his fellow Christians. He wants others to know just where he stands in relation to God.

Baptism includes striving daily to please God. Every day the Christian remembers the new life God grants to him. This new life is a new kind of living. But no Christian can live a perfect life. This new life is the power of God to disown the sinful nature and to seek that which God offers in His Word. God enables him to love his fellowmen. God's Spirit gives him the power to confess that Jesus is his Lord. Paul describes Jesus' lordship in these words:

For the love of Christ controls us because we are convinced that One has died for all; therefore all have died. And He died for all, that those who live might live no longer for themselves but for Him who for their sake died and was raised. *2 Corinthians 5:14-15*

236

THE CHRISTIAN BELIEVES: **My Baptism Is God's Own Personal Covenant Promising to Give Me Forgiveness and Eternal Life**

My baptism marks the beginning of my life of repentance for my sins, my faith in Jesus Christ, and my living a godly life. I am committed to my Lord's death and resurrection. Daily I drown my old Adam in repentance. Daily the Lord Jesus takes over my life so the new man can praise God.

My baptism is my assurance that God's Holy Spirit will keep me by His grace in the true faith. My Lord gives me victory in my struggles with sin. God will bring me safely into eternal glory when I die.

These are the reasons why I want to praise God for my baptism every day of my life.

Prayer Thought—

I ask God to lead me to daily repentance.
I call upon Him to uphold me as I battle
against the old Adam and seek a
righteous life.

With one accord, O God, we pray:
Grant us Thy Holy Spirit;
Look Thou on our infirmity
Through Jesus' blood and merit.
Grant us to grow in grace each day
That by this Sacrament we may
Eternal life inherit.

Hymn 301, stanza 2

51

What Is the Sacrament of the Altar?

While the people of Israel traveled through the desert to the Promised Land, God gave them provisions for the way. Manna, quail, and water sustained them.

God's people are still pilgrims. They are on the way to the promised land of heaven. Through Baptism God continually adds to the number of His people. To sustain them on the way He has given His Word in the Bible. In addition, He has provided another wonderful sacrament. This is *The Sacrament of the Altar,* also called *Holy Communion.*

What is Holy Communion?
Holy Communion is the body and blood of our Lord Jesus Christ given with bread and wine, instituted by Christ Himself for us to eat and drink.

Where do the Scriptures say this?
Matthew, Mark, Luke, and Paul say: Our Lord Jesus Christ, in the night in which He was betrayed, took bread; and when He had given thanks, He broke it and gave it to His disciples, saying, "Take, eat; this is My body, which is given for you; this do in remembrance of Me." After the same manner also He took the cup after supper, and when He had given thanks, He gave it to them, saying, "Drink of it, all of you; this cup is the new testament in My blood, which is shed for you and for many for the remission of sins; this do, as often as you drink it, in remembrance of Me."

THIS IS THE CHRISTIAN FAITH: In the Sacrament of the Altar Jesus Gives Us His Body and His Blood

On the Thursday evening before He died Jesus celebrated the Passover with His apostles. In this celebration they remembered how the angel of death had passed over the homes of the Israelites in Egypt. They told

again how the blood of an innocent lamb on the doorpost was the sign of God's people. Now on the next day the *true* Lamb of God was to die on the cross to deliver men from eternal death. That His people might be forever connected to the sacrifice on Calvary, Jesus gave the Sacrament of the Altar. At His command and invitation God's people have celebrated that sacrament ever since.

Jesus shared bread and wine with His friends. These are visible in the Sacrament. The wonder is that under the bread and wine Jesus' body and blood are *really present*. Faith in God's power leads His people to accept the real presence of the Lord's body and blood in the Sacrament. With the voice of faith they confess:

> ✠ Now to Him who by the power at work within us is able to do far more abundantly than all that we ask or think, to Him be glory in the church. *Ephesians 3:20-21a*

Each person who comes to the Sacrament receives: bread, wine, Christ's body, and Christ's blood. The bread and wine are not merely symbols of the body and blood. Nor are the bread and wine changed into flesh and blood. St. Paul clearly speaks of four elements in the Sacrament:

> ✠ The cup of blessing which we bless, is it not a participation in the blood of Christ? The bread which we break, is it not a participation in the body of Christ? *1 Corinthians 10:16*

Jesus' words show that the Sacrament is to be *eaten* and *drunk* in the sacred ceremony. Mistaken people may do strange things with it. The bread and wine of the Sacrament are not to be worshiped.

God's people call this sacrament by several names. It is the "Lord's Supper" because the Lord gave it. It is the "Sacrament of the Altar" because the visible elements are placed on the altar in church. It is the "Eucharist" because Christians always give thanks for its blessings. It is "Holy Communion" because it is a union of bread and wine with the body and blood of Christ. Also, in it God's people are united with Christ and with one another.

The Sacrament of the Altar is a remembrance. Each time God's people celebrate it, they proclaim the good news of Jesus' death that men might live. St. Paul writes:

> ✠ For as often as you eat this bread and drink the cup, you proclaim the Lord's death until He comes. *1 Corinthians 11:26*

The Sacrament of the Altar is placed between "the Lord's death" and "the Lord's coming." Behind the Sacrament is the cross. Jesus made His sacrifice once for all. He does not repeat His sacrifice. He does, however, offer the benefits of His great sacrifice again and again. In this way the Sacrament sustains the Christians' faith until the Lord returns in glory.

The Passover blood sealed a covenant in which God promised to protect His people. The Sacrament also seals a covenant or testament. It seals and carries to God's people His forgiving love and eternal protection. Christians are drawn by the sin of this earth, yet they reach for heaven. In the Sacrament God lifts them heavenward.

THE CHRISTIAN BELIEVES: Christ Sustains Me by His Holy Supper

How vast the difference between the holy God and my sinful self! Yet my God has claimed me. He has come to me because I cannot come to Him by my own ability.

In His Sacrament of the Altar I see another proof of His grace. He gives me His body! He gives me His blood! With urgent invitation and promise of forgiveness He meets my sin and weakness. How blessed are the people of God!

Prayer Thought—

Scripture's teaching about the Lord's Supper is far beyond my ability to understand. I earnestly pray for faith in the mystery and power of this sacrament.

An awe-full mystery is here
To challenge faith and waken fear:
The Savior comes as food divine,
Concealed in earthly bread and wine.

In consecrated wine and bread
No eye perceives the mystery dread;
But Jesus' words are strong and clear:
"My body and My blood are here."

Hymn 304, stanzas 1 and 3

241

52

The Blessings and Power of the Lord's Supper

You don't get much to eat or drink in the Lord's Supper. At other meals there may be much food. But in this sacramental meal you get only a thin wafer and sip of wine.

But then, this meal isn't meant for bodily hunger. This sacrament nourishes our life in God. The Lord Himself left no doubt about the *Benefits of the Lord's Supper.*

What benefits do we receive from this sacrament?
The benefits of this sacrament are pointed out by the words, *given and shed for you for the remission of sins.* These words assure us that in the sacrament we receive forgiveness of sins, life, and salvation. For where there is forgiveness of sins, there is also life and salvation.

How can eating and drinking do all this?
It is not eating and drinking that does this, but the words, *given and shed for you for the remission of sins.* These words, along with eating and drinking, are the main thing in the sacrament. And whoever believes these words has exactly what they say, forgiveness of sins.

THIS IS THE CHRISTIAN FAITH: **God's Word in the Sacrament Gives Eternal Blessings to Believers**

What does God offer in the Sacrament? He offers these great blessings. In the Sacrament God offers *forgiveness of sins.* This does not mean that Jesus' death on Calvary was not needed. On the cross Jesus bore the sins of all men. He won forgiveness. This is the forgiveness which God offers in the Sacrament. When God pardons sins, He gives great benefits to the believer.

In the Sacrament God offers *life.* This is the result of freedom from the guilt and burden of our sin. When a physician takes away disease, he

gives health. In God's view anyone whose sins are not forgiven does not have life. He may move about. His body and mind work. However, unless he is at peace with God, God counts Him as dead. The unforgiven person does not even know what it feels like to be really alive. He can't appreciate the life of love and hope. To live each day as a child of God — this is *real* life, spiritual life. God offers to lift the burden of sin and says through Paul:

> You also must consider yourselves dead to sin and alive to God in Christ Jesus. *Romans 6:11*

Living each day as a forgiven child of God, the Christian is ready for death or the Lord's coming. The gift of life leads to life forever.

In the Sacrament God offers *salvation*. At the judgment the believer will stand unafraid. No sins bar his way to heaven. Thus the blessing of Jesus' cross continues through life to the very gate of heaven. St. Paul showed how one divine gift leads to another:

> But now that you have been set free from sin and have become slaves of God, the return you get is sanctification and its end, eternal life. *Romans 6:22*

These gifts God offers in several ways. He offers them in Baptism; He offers them in the study of His Word; in the Lord's Supper He gives the body and blood of His Son as His pledge. Here He comes to each individual believer. At Baptism a Christian may be too young to sense God's coming. When the Word is taught, a person might miss the point that the promises are for *him*. In the Lord's Supper there is no doubt. As he receives the elements, the Christian hears the words FOR YOU. He is directly and personally assured that Christ died for him.

The *power* of the Lord's Supper is the same as the power of Baptism. On the one hand, there is God's Word. It is not a vague promise. Jesus says exactly what He means: "This is My body and blood given and shed for the remission of sins." When Jesus says those words, He does what He says. God's Son gave up His life to pay the price for man's sin. He arose to show that He was true God and had defeated sin and death.

The Sacrament of the Altar is a personal meeting of two people. There is the living Lord with His unbreakable promise. There is the sinner. The sinner must be there not only in body to partake of the bread and wine. He must be there in faith. He must accept the gifts. "He that *believes* these words has what they say and express, namely, the forgiveness of sins." As the believer receives the body and blood, he is joined to his

Lord. From his Lord flows life and power to believe in and love Him. Jesus desires this closeness. He says:

> ✠ I am the Vine, you are the branches. He who abides in Me and I in him, he it is that bears much fruit, for apart from Me you can do nothing.
>
> *John 15:5*

THE CHRISTIAN BELIEVES: God's Word in the Sacrament Strengthens My Faith for Time and Eternity

My faith is constantly under attack. From within me doubts and worldly lusts tear at my faith. From without temptations lay siege. How shall I remain a child of God?

In my baptism my Lord called me into His kingdom. Through the hearing of His Word He has strengthened my faith. As He graciously gives me His body and blood to assure me, He draws me close to Himself. At the Communion rail I will hear Him say to me: "My body, My blood, for the forgiveness of *your* sins, dear one."

Prayer Thought—

I thank the Lord for offering such great benefits in the Sacrament. I pray for faith that I may receive that for which He has paid so costly a price.

He who craves a precious treasure
Neither cost nor pain will measure;
But the priceless gifts of heaven
God to us hath freely given.
Though the wealth of earth were proffered,
Naught could buy the gifts here offered:
Christ's true body, for thee riven,
And His blood, for thee once given.

Hymn 305, stanza 3

53

Getting Ready for the Sacrament

People are usually careful about the solemn events of life. They get ready for them. The bride and groom rehearse their wedding service. Ladies practice to curtsy before a queen.

God's people prepare both their bodies and their hearts when they worship God in church. The Lord has told His followers to prepare with special care when they come to His Holy Supper. This is a solemn and holy act. Christians are concerned about the proper use of the *Lord's Supper*.

> When is a person rightly prepared to receive this sacrament?
> Fasting and other outward preparations serve a good purpose. However, that person is well prepared and worthy who believes these words, *given and shed for you for the remission of sins.* But anyone who does not believe these words, or doubts them, is neither prepared nor worthy, for the words *for you* require simply a believing heart.

THIS IS THE CHRISTIAN FAITH: The Benefits of the Lord's Supper Come to Those Who Are Properly Prepared

Those who come to the Sacrament prepare their bodies. They honor God by being neat and clean. Some even go without food for a while to remind themselves to think about God and His mercies.

The Christian uses these bodily preparations to lead him to the more important preparations of the soul. He is ready if he believes Jesus' promise to forgive his sins. No one attends a concert wearing ear plugs. No one wears a blindfold to a movie. It is worse to go to Holy Communion with a closed heart. The gifts of God are in the Sacrament, but he who does not believe cannot receive them. If a person has faith in his heart, he is ready. Faith opens his eyes to his sinfulness. Faith helps him see God against whom he sins.

Only those who are ready should come to the Lord's Supper. There is a good reason for this. The Lord tells us through St. Paul:

 Whoever, therefore, eats the bread or drinks the cup of the Lord in an unworthy manner will be guilty of profaning the body and blood of the Lord. . . . For anyone who eats and drinks without discerning the body eats and drinks judgment upon himself.

1 Corinthians 11:27, 29

If a person takes the bread and wine in the Sacrament, he receives the body and blood of the Lord *whether he believes it or not.* However, if he does not believe that the Lord's body and blood are present, he is not worthy to partake. If he doubts that Jesus offers him the forgiveness of sins, he is calling God a liar. He does not receive a blessing. He adds to his sins by dishonoring God. He brings God's judgment upon himself.

Certain people, then, should not participate in the Sacrament. Those who are still deliberately living in sin should not come. They cannot repent and seek forgiveness as long as they want to sin. Also those who have hurt another person by word or deed and have not made it right are not ready for the Sacrament. Jesus warned:

 So if you are offering your gift at the altar and there remember that your brother has something against you, leave your gift before the altar and go; first be reconciled to your brother, and then come and offer your gift.

Matthew 5:23-24

247

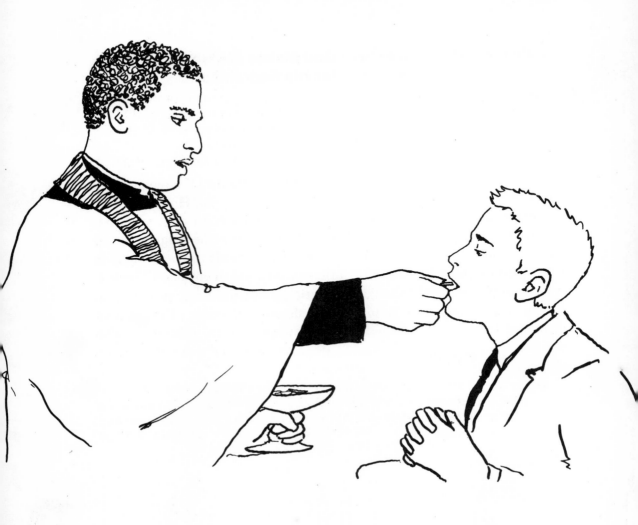

It would be well if all confessing Christians could come together to the Sacrament. Some, however, believe falsely about God. Some have been taught wrongly. Some stubbornly ignore the Bible's teachings and believe their own ideas. To come to Holy Communion together, people should believe and confess a common faith in God's act of grace. Close Communion is the practice of allowing only those to come to the Lord's Table who have made this common confession of faith.

Not every Christian has a strong faith. Many have doubts and fears. They long for the Sacrament that their weak faith may be strengthened. The Lord especially invites them. Isaiah says of God:

> A bruised reed He will not break, and a dimly burning wick He will not quench.
> *Isaiah 42:3*

248

THE CHRISTIAN BELIEVES: God Makes Me Ready for His Sacrament

Jesus is truly present in the celebration of His Holy Supper! How exciting it is to know that He makes every guest at His Table today a member of His first Supper. I want to be prepared for this great event, as Paul says:

> Let a man examine himself and so eat of the bread and drink of the cup.
> *1 Corinthians 11:28*

I am prepared when God gives me faith. In faith I see my sinfulness and the judgment of God. In faith I see God's grace and mercy in Jesus Christ. I believe in Him and His promise to give me forgiveness and life in the Holy Supper. I am worthy and well prepared when I look only to Jesus for mercy. I want to be His guest many times.

Prayer Thought—

I ask God for faith to see my sinfulness.
I ask God for strength to repent and live
His life. I thank Him for the gift of His
Holy Supper. I pray that I may partake of
it worthily many times.

Oh, grant that I in manner worthy
May now approach Thy heavenly Board
And, as I lowly bow before Thee,
Look only unto Thee, O Lord!
Lord, may Thy body and Thy blood
Be for my soul the highest good!

Hymn 315, stanza 2

54

Claiming God's Promises

What kind of a father would give his child a stone for a piece of bread? or a snake for a fish?

This sounds strange to us. Jesus used these questions to make an important point. He said:

> "If you then, who are evil, know how to give good gifts to your children, how much more will your Father who is in heaven give good gifts to those who ask Him!" *Matthew 7:11*

> "What man of you, if his son asks him for bread, will give him a stone? Or if he asks for a fish, will give him a serpent?" *Matthew 7:9-10*

We cannot imagine a faithful father deceiving his child in such a way. So much the more reason for Christians to trust their heavenly Father. Jesus urges His followers to be bold in their prayers and requests to God:

> ✠ "Ask, and it will be given you; seek and you will find; knock, and it will be opened to you." *Matthew 7:7*

God offers so much to His children, as we have seen in the lessons on the sacraments. God wants His children to claim these blessings boldly and confidently.

THIS IS THE CHRISTIAN FAITH: The Almighty God Stands Behind His Promises for Life

When the Christian faces the judgment of God, he feels small. He knows that He does not earn the goodness of God. He admits that he really deserves punishment and death. He confesses with Jacob:

> ✠ "I am not worthy of the least of all the steadfast love and all the faithfulness which Thou hast shown to Thy servant." *Genesis 32:10*

To the Christian who feels helpless and worthless, God's Gospel promises come as the greatest news there is. The Bible becomes the Christian's most precious book because it brings these promises of God to him. Through Isaiah God promises:

> "Though your sins are like scarlet, they shall be as white as snow; though they are red like crimson, they shall become like wool."
>
> *Isaiah 1:18b*

> ✠ "For the mountains may depart and the hills be removed, but My steadfast love shall not depart from you, and My covenant of peace shall not be removed, says the Lord, who has compassion on you."
>
> *Isaiah 54:10*

Jesus Christ is the living Word of God. When He spoke, He spoke God's Word. Listen to His great promises:

> "Come to Me, all who labor and are heavy laden, and I will give you rest."
>
> *Matthew 11:28*

> "Him who comes to Me I will not cast out." *John 6:37b*

> "Truly, truly, I say to you, if you ask anything of the Father, He will give it to you in My name."
>
> *John 16:23b*

Jesus' entire life, death, and resurrection is God's great "Yes!" to His promises to us. God keeps these promises forever. St. Paul said:

> ✠ For all the promises of God find their Yes in Him.
>
> *2 Corinthians 1:20a*

How do Christians claim God's promises? St. Paul answers this question in these words to his congregation at Philippi:

> Work out your own salvation with fear and trembling; for God is at work in you both to will and to work for His good pleasure.
>
> *Philippians 2:12b-13*

God has given His means of grace. Through them He brings His church the blessings of His love. As the Christian uses these means in his daily life God's Spirit is active within him.

The Christian remembers God's continual forgiveness in Christ when he thinks of his baptism. Christian parents gladly bring their infant sons and daughters to God in Baptism. The Christian uses every opportunity to hear God's Word in church, in catechism class, and in family worship. A child of God partakes of Holy Communion regularly and often.

Every time the Christian meets God in worship, in prayer, in Word and in the Sacrament, he is claiming God's promises for himself.

THE CHRISTIAN BELIEVES: God Keeps His Promises to Me

When I find myself trapped by Satan's temptations, it is my own fault. It is because I turned my back on God and His Word. I did not pay attention to Him. I did not turn to Him in my guilt.

God promises me forgiveness in Jesus Christ. God keeps this promise. He calls me again and again by His Gospel. He assures me of His steadfast love. He promises that no one can take me away from His loving care.

God's Spirit works in me to make me a witness of God's faithfulness. I pray that other people may be led to my Lord by my witness.

Prayer Thought—

I ask God to forgive me when I am
careless in coming to Him for His gifts.
I praise God for His steadfast love and
faithfulness. I ask Him to give me
confidence and trust in Him alone.

Help us that we Thy saving Word
In faithful hearts may treasure;
Let e'er that Bread of Life afford
New grace in richest measure.
Yea, let us die to every sin,
For heaven create us new within
That fruits of faith may flourish.

Hymn 293, stanza 2

55

Ambassadors for Christ

An ambassador is the representative of his government in another country. He deserves the respect and honor which his country should receive. He speaks for the highest officials of his country.

This is an example of the power which God gives to His church. Jesus commissioned all His disciples to be His spokesmen, His ambassadors. This lesson explains this commission in the answer to the question regarding the *Office of the Keys*.

What is the "Office of the Keys"?
It is that authority which Christ gave to His church to forgive the sins of those who repent and to declare to those who do not repent that their sins are not forgiven.

What are the words of Christ?
Our Lord Jesus Christ said to His disciples: "Receive the Holy Spirit. If you forgive the sins of any, they are forgiven; if you retain the sins of any, they are retained." (John 20:23)

"Truly, I say to you, Whatever you bind on earth shall be bound in heaven, and whatever you loose on earth shall be loosed in heaven." (Matthew 18:18)

THIS IS THE CHRISTIAN FAITH: God's People Have the Power and Duty to Bring the Gospel into the Lives of Other People

St. Paul describes the work and message of God's ambassadors.

All this is from God, who through Christ reconciled us to Himself and gave us the ministry of reconciliation; that is, God was in Christ reconciling the world to Himself, not counting their trespasses against them, and entrusting to us the message of reconciliation. So we are ambassadors for Christ, God making His appeal through us. We beseech you on behalf of Christ, be reconciled to God.

2 Corinthians 5:18-20

254

The message is the Gospel. It is God's Word which shows men that they cannot justify themselves. It is God's Word which tells men what God did for them in Christ. This is the most important message there is.

God has entrusted this message to His disciples. We are God's spokesmen. God uses us to make His appeal to men. God's Spirit works through us to bring forgiveness to sinners.

Jesus tells His disciples that the Word or message would be the keys of the kingdom of heaven. Some will hear the Gospel spoken by ambassadors and will believe. God will forgive the sin of the penitent and thus they will be "loosed" from sin's guilt and power. But there may be others who will not believe when they hear the Gospel. They will remain "bound" in their sins. Jesus said:

> ✠ I will give you the keys of the kingdom of heaven, and whatever you bind on earth shall be bound in heaven, and whatever you loose on earth shall be loosed in heaven.　*Matthew 16:19*

This proclaiming of the Word of God is called the "peculiar church power." It is a *special* power given only to God's people, who are the body of Christ.

This God-given responsibility of proclaiming the Gospel rests upon each Christian. God has no other plan for getting His grace to sinners. He honors His people for doing His work. Their glory is seen as God says:

> ✠ But you are a chosen race, a royal priesthood, a holy nation, God's own people, that you may declare the wonderful deeds of Him who called you out of darkness into His marvelous light.   *1 Peter 2:9*

Each Christian seeks ways to carry out this task. He uses opportunities to witness about Jesus to others. At the risk of being despised, he boldly confesses his faith. Many have died for doing this.

Because the task is so great, Christians join together in the work. Church membership is not an escape from the world. It is a way by which Christians can do together what they cannot do alone.

Congregations can conduct worship services. They can invite unbelievers to hear the Gospel. They operate schools to teach the Word. They administer Baptism and celebrate the Lord's Supper. They go to the homes in their towns and cities to bring the Good News to those who will not come to hear it.

Because not even a large congregation can go to all the world, congregations join in groups called a *synod*. Together, thousands of Christians can spread the Gospel to all the world. They combine their money. They build colleges to train workers. They send some of their fellow members to go for them to distant lands. They print and distribute Bibles and books. They train each other to be better witnesses and workers.

THE CHRISTIAN BELIEVES: I Am an Ambassador for Christ

God has called me to be His own. To all eternity I am one of God's people. As such I have a task and assignment from God. In faith I accept my assignment. With God's help I will confess Christ and tell of His grace. I will use my time and toil, my treasure and talent for His kingdom. With my fellow Christians I live as a royal priest of God and bring forgiveness and life to the world.

I ask God to keep me aware of my
responsibility to apply His grace to others.
I ask Him to give me courage, generosity,
and skill to be a worthy witness.

Soldiers of the Cross, arise,
Gird you with your armor bright.
Mighty are your enemies,
Hard the battle ye must fight.

Mid the homes of want and woe,
Strangers to the living Word,
Let the Savior's heralds go,
Let the voice of hope be heard.

Hymn 501, stanzas 1 and 3

257

56

The Special Ministry

Every Christian is a minister. Each believer is appointed by God to "minister," or serve, in spreading the Gospel of Christ. In his own place in life each child of God has opportunities to work for Christ's kingdom.

In addition, the Head of the church has arranged for special ministries. When God's people form congregations, they need people who can guide and lead. Not all Christians are able to preach and teach. Christians would probably have decided for themselves that they needed trained and gifted leaders, but from the beginning of the church the Lord established the *Office of the Keys* and ordained the office of the special ministry. Some editions of the Catechism include the following:

What do you believe according to these words?
I believe that when the called ministers of Christ deal with us by His divine command, especially when they exclude manifest and impenitent sinners from the Christian congregation, and, again, when they absolve those who repent of their sins and are willing to amend, this is as valid and certain, in heaven also, as if Christ, our dear Lord, dealt with us Himself.

THIS IS THE CHRISTIAN FAITH: God Gives to His Church
Special Ministers to
Lead and Train His People

God ordained the special ministry. He told His people to choose, with His guidance, people who are able to act for them and teach them. He did not mean that His people were to hire men to do all of the church work for them.

On behalf of the congregation the special ministers of the church preach in the public services; they baptize; they celebrate Holy Communion; they teach; they pronounce God's forgiveness or withhold it from unrepentant sinners. They help God's people to plan and carry out a busy program of Kingdom work.

259

When the special ministers do these things, they are not acting for themselves. They speak and act in place of their people and in place of God. What they do, then, is valid when they speak the Word of God. Saint Paul gives an example. Jesus had made him an apostle and had permitted him to start the congregation in Corinth. Of his work there Paul wrote:

> What I have forgiven, if I have forgiven anything, has been for your sake in the presence of Christ. *2 Corinthians 2:10b*

St. Paul describes the special minister in these words:

> This is how one should regard us, as servants of Christ and stewards of the mysteries of God. Moreover it is required of stewards that they be found trustworthy. *1 Corinthians 4:1-2*

That God is active in giving such leaders to the church is shown by Paul's words:

> And His gifts were that some should be apostles, some prophets, some evangelists, some pastors and teachers. *Ephesians 4:11*

The special ministers come from among God's people. Promising young people prepare themselves for the special ministry. The congregations join together to maintain colleges where the skills needed by the church can be taught. After training, people are ready for a "call." Praying fervently, a congregation which needs a leader formally asks a qualified Christian to be its pastor, teacher, or other leader. In accepting the call, the person knows that God has placed him in his work. All special ministers are instructed:

> Take heed to yourselves and to all the flock, in which the Holy Spirit has made you guardians. *Acts 20:28a*

To do God's work, the church needs many kinds of special ministers. It needs pastors to teach, preach, administer the sacraments, and speak God's forgiveness. It needs teachers for its schools. It needs professors for its colleges. It needs some people to teach part time in Sunday school. It needs missionaries and executives. It needs trained youth workers. It needs women to serve as deaconesses. It needs chaplains in the armed services and in hospitals and jails. All these we call "church vocations."

God's people do not give up their rights when they call special ministers. The special ministers do not own the congregations. They are not set above God's people. Christians are grateful for their special ministers. They know God gives leaders —

> for the equipment of the saints, for the work of ministry, for building up the body of Christ. *Ephesians 4:12*

260

Christians work with their leaders. They come to hear their pastors preach. To their leaders they say: "Here we are. Equip us and help us see and do our work for Christ." Since the special ministers proclaim God's Word, their people honor them. In love and respect the people care for the bodily needs of pastors and teachers.

THE CHRISTIAN BELIEVES: **My Pastor and Teachers Are God's Gifts to Help Me in My Ministry as a Christian**

In my own life God has helped me through my pastor and teachers. By speaking God's Word they have led me to faith and knowledge of Christ.

As a child of God I will honor the special ministers He provides. I will work with them. In honoring and obeying them, I will show my respect and love for God. In planning my life, I will seriously think about preparing myself to serve as a special minister. God may someday call me through a group of His Christians.

Prayer Thought—

> I ask God to help me accept thankfully
> the work of my pastors and teachers as
> a gift from Him. I ask Him to bless and
> uphold all special ministers of the Gospel.

> Lord of the Church, we humbly pray
> For those who guide us in Thy way
> And speak Thy holy Word.
> With love divine their hearts inspire
> And touch their lips with hallowed fire
> And needful strength afford.
>
> *Hymn 489, stanza 1*

57

Mutual Care and Discipline

Do Christians sometimes put people out of the church? In the section of the Catechism which we have just studied, we read: "When they exclude manifest and impenitent sinners from the Christian congregation." Yes, occasionally the sad day comes when God's people must say to a fellow member, "You do not have the marks of a Christian."

This does not happen to every Christian who sins. If it did, no one would remain in the church. All Christians are sinners. Jesus founded the church so that sinners could learn how serious their sins are. In the church He offers the forgiveness which He earned.

It is the responsibility of Christians to help each other repent and accept the forgiveness of God. Mostly they do this as they regularly teach the Law and the Gospel and administer the sacraments to each other. If a fellow Christian does *not* repent, it becomes the duty of God's people to deal with him directly. The Lord has given careful instructions about how to do this.

THIS IS THE CHRISTIAN FAITH: God Charges His People to Win Their Fallen Brothers Back to Faith

In dealing with a Christian who openly and repeatedly sins, the first rule is: "Be patient." As forgiven sinners, Christians sympathize with other sinners and show concern when a brother or sister in the faith sins. They are not to think: "That's his business if he wants to sin. I don't want to get into an argument." As unpleasant as it may be to try to help a fellow sinner, God makes each Christian his brother's keeper, saying:

> And we exhort you, brethren, admonish the idle, encourage the fainthearted, help the weak, be patient with them all.
>
> *1 Thessalonians 5:14*

263

Jesus urges us to do everything we can to help an erring brother:

✠ If your brother sins against you, go and tell him his fault between you and him alone. If he listens to you, you have gained your brother. But if he does not listen, take one or two others along with you, that every word may be confirmed by the evidence of two or three witnesses. If he refuses to listen to them, tell it to the church; and if he refuses to listen even to the church, let him be to you as a Gentile and a tax collector. *Matthew 18:15-17*

In these steps, what do Christians say to the sinner? In gentle words they speak the Law to him. They ask him to admit his sin and to admit that it *is* sin. They point out the judgment of God upon unrepentant sinners. If he does repent, they speak the Gospel. If he confesses and believes the Gospel, any fellow Christian may tell him that for Jesus' sake his sins are forgiven.

In all this the purpose is not to drive a sinner away. It is meant to save him. When brotherly admonition succeeds, there is rejoicing, even among God's angels. The sin is forgotten and never held against the repentant Christian.

If he refuses to repent, the church sadly announces that the efforts have failed.

Even then all is not finished. God's people continue to work. If ever the sinner repents, he is welcomed back. Until he does repent, however, he cannot have the privileges of a Christian. He cannot receive the Lord's Supper. He cannot serve as a sponsor at a baptism. He will not be buried as a Christian. But he *is* urged to attend worship services, and fellow Christians never stop trying to win him back. They want to keep speaking the Word of God to him.

There is no time or number limit on forgiveness. As often as a Christian sins and repents, his Savior forgives. God's people can do no less. Peter once asked if seven times was enough to forgive a sinner. Jesus said, "I do not say to you seven times but seventy times seven."

Christians are not to resent it when their pastor or fellow Christians tell them they have sinned. They are to expect it and be grateful for it. Discipline in the church is God's plan to have His people protect each other, as He says:

✠ If anyone among you wanders from the truth and someone brings him back, let him know that whoever brings back a sinner from the error of his way will save his soul from death and will cover a multitude of sins. *James 5:19-20*

It is easy to see that this plan requires real Christian love. If people try to criticize in pride or simply try to get rid of someone, hatred can develop. Calling to repentance is the special work of God through the preaching of Law and Gospel.

THE CHRISTIAN BELIEVES: Brotherly Admonition Is a Benefit and a Duty for Me

Brotherly admonition is a benefit. My fellow Christians care about me. Satan is a strong enemy. Left to myself, I might fall from faith. I recognize God's protecting hand when my pastor or Christian friends admonish me. The Lord is my Keeper. Often He uses other believers to uphold me when I am weak.

Brotherly admonition is also my duty. Every fellow Christian is my concern. I will not hesitate to bring back, with love and courage, a fellow Christian who falls. This I will do with humility and patience. I too am a forgiven sinner.

Prayer Thought—

I thank God for making my fellow
Christians watchmen of my soul. I ask
God for wisdom to receive admonition as
a blessing. I also ask Him to show me my
duty to brothers and sisters in Christ.
I pray for a kind heart and gentle speech
to admonish others in the spirit of Christ.

In the hour of trial
Jesus, plead for me
Lest by base denial
I depart from Thee.
When Thou seest me waver,
With a look recall
Nor for fear or favor
Suffer me to fall.

Hymn 516, stanza 1

265

58

Confession and Absolution

A sick child in a family receives the special care and concern of his parents. However, wise parents do not neglect the other children of the family. They too need regular attention and guidance.

In a Christian congregation God's people are deeply concerned about *impenitent* sinners. In Christian admonition and mutual care the congregation goes into action for the sake of one another. Meanwhile, the *penitent* sinners are not forgotten. The Word and the sacraments are continually brought to them. All of God's people need to bring their sinful lives before the light of God's law. Repeatedly they need to have the Gospel applied to their penitent hearts. To encourage all Christians in the constant use of Word and sacrament, God has provided the arrangement called *confession*.

What is private confession?

Private confession has two parts. First, we make a personal confession of sins to the pastor, and then we receive absolution, which means forgiveness as from God Himself. This absolution we should not doubt, but firmly believe that thereby our sins are forgiven before God in heaven.

What sins should we confess?

Before God we should confess that we are guilty of all sins, even those which are not known to us, as we do in the Lord's Prayer. But in private confession, as before the pastor, we should confess only those sins which trouble us in heart and mind.

What are such sins?

We can examine our everyday life according to the Ten Commandments—for example, how we act toward father or mother, son or daughter, husband or wife, or toward the people with whom we work, and so on. We may ask ourselves whether we have been disobedient or unfaithful, bad-tempered or dishonest, or whether we have hurt anyone by word or deed.

THIS IS THE CHRISTIAN FAITH:
In Confession and Absolution Christians Continually Turn from Sin to God's Forgiveness in Baptism

To confess means to admit sin. It means to stand under the judgment of God's law, which convicts a sinner. His sin separates him from God. He is anxious to get rid of the guilt of his sin. He confesses so that he may hear again the good news that God forgives. He seeks strength to keep from sinning again. For Jesus' sake God is willing and able to answer the cry of the confessing Christian.

> ✠ If we say we have no sin we deceive ourselves, and the truth is not in us. If we confess our sins, He is faithful and just and will forgive our sins and cleanse us from all unrighteousness. *1 John 1:8-9*

God has committed the use of the Word and the sacraments to His believers. Therefore the Christian can go to a fellow Christian and hear the actual words of absolution: "You are forgiven." Often the pastor will say the words. When the words are said, they count as much as if God spoke directly from heaven. This assurance of forgiveness is "absolution."

There are several ways in which a Christian may or should confess.

The Christian may always confess *directly to the open ear of God.* The psalmist speaks for all Christians when he reports:

> I acknowledged my sin to Thee, and I did not hide my iniquity; I said, "I will confess my transgressions to the Lord"; then Thou didst forgive the guilt of my sin. *Psalm 32:5*

Christians also use the privilege of *helping each other confess.* The Scriptures encourage this.

> Therefore confess your sins to one another, and pray for one another that you may be healed. *James 5:16a*

When a Christian has hurt anyone, he confesses this *to the person he has injured.* God's people readily forgive each other. They are more concerned for the person who has sinned than they are for their own pride.

In the public church services, God's people provide opportunities for confession. They join hearts and lips in a general confession, using words which fit all sinners. Again they rejoice to hear the pastor say, "In the name of Christ, I forgive you."

Each Christian has the special privilege of confessing *to his pastor.* He is not forced to do this. In privacy a Christian may confess his sins in detail. Before his pastor he bares those sins which especially trouble him.

The pastor's absolution in Christ's name brings peace to the sinner's heart. The absolution helps him avoid sin. The pastor is not permitted to reveal any matter which has been confided to him in private confession. To encourage people to use private confession, pastors set aside a time and have a quiet place where no one else may hear. A pastor does not pry into sins. He simply stands in the place of God to offer help when it is requested.

God's people do not look upon confession as an unpleasant duty. They know that at the end of every sincere confession they will hear their Savior say:

Take heart, My son; your sins are forgiven. *Matthew 9:2b*

THE CHRISTIAN BELIEVES: By Confession and Absolution I Draw Near to My God for Cleansing Each Day

As a baptized, redeemed child of God I have an open door to God's love and mercy. He knows my sins before I tell Him. Yet He invites me to unburden myself and receive His assuring words, as they may be spoken by my pastor or a fellow Christian. I will therefore take advantage of His invitation. Daily I will confess in prayer. When a sin burdens me, I will use the privilege of confessing to my pastor. He will speak the absolution to me personally.

Prayer Thought—

> I ask God to make me aware of my own sins. I thank Him for forgiving me for Jesus' sake. I ask for a true faith in His words of absolution.

> I, a sinner, come to Thee
> With a penitent confession;
> Savior, mercy show to me,
> Grant for all my sins remission.
> Let these words my soul relieve:
> Jesus sinners doth receive.
>
> *Hymn 324, stanza 5*

"Christ who is our life"
Colossians 3:4

Section VI: Living for Jesus

59. **The Fruit of the Spirit in the Christian Life**
60. **Growing as a Christian**
61. **The Christian Life of Worship**
62. **Living Witnesses of the Living Lord**

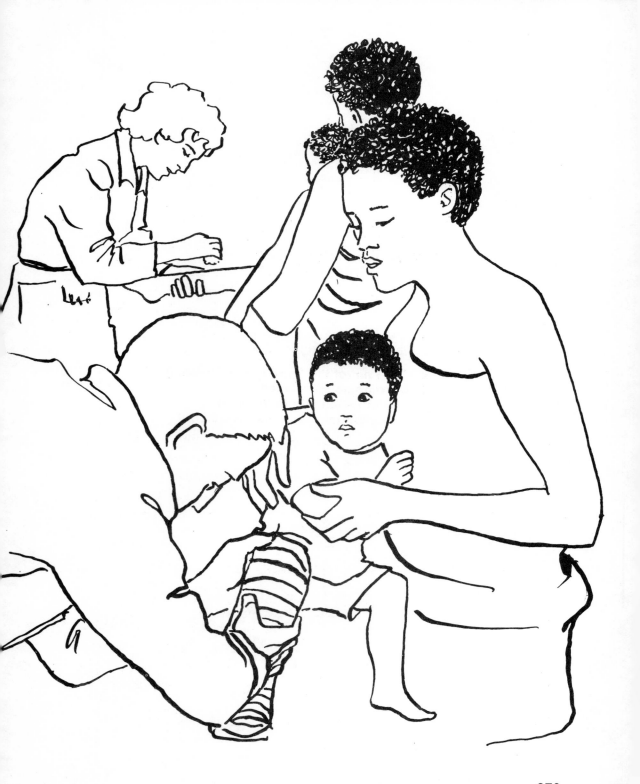

The Fruits of the Spirit in the Christian Life

To have good fruits, a tree must have good roots. The same is true of the Christian. If his faith is firmly embedded in God's truth and mercy, he will be able to produce the fruits of good works. Faith and deeds belong to-gether—but in their proper order.

WE ARE SAVED BY GRACE, NOT BY WORKS

False religions *begin* with good works. They teach that men can satisfy God with their own deeds. They do not agree on how many or what kind of good deeds are required. Some think it is enough just to mean well. At the other extreme, some even demand human sacrifices.

The Christian religion begins by teaching that no man can ever do enough to satisfy God's righteousness. By nature men can't stop dis-pleasing God. God Himself gave His Son as the only acceptable sacrifice. Salvation is all God's doing.

> For by grace you have been saved through faith; and this is not your own doing, it is the gift of God—not because of works, lest any man should boast. *Ephesians 2:8-9*

GOD MAKES PEOPLE ABLE TO DO GOOD WORKS

God's gracious plan of salvation is all-inclusive. He is responsible for starting the plan. He gave His only-begotten Son to carry out its require-ments. Our Lord Jesus is God's living Word of love for all sinners. Through Him God reconciled the world to Himself, not counting their sins against them.

God does more. He sends His Holy Spirit to bring all the blessings of His grace and love to sinful human beings. By the Gospel the Spirit changes men's lives. He changes them from enemies of God to disciples of Christ. He frees them from slavery to sin and makes them free under the Gospel. He raises spiritually dead people to a new life. Paul says:

> ✠ If anyone is in Christ, he is a new creation; the old has passed away, behold, the new has come. *2 Corinthians 5:17*

This is all God's own work. Man cannot devise good of himself. Any good that a child of God does is the result of God's Spirit within him. The apostle makes this point very clear in writing to the Ephesians:

> ✠ We are His workmanship, created in Christ Jesus for good works, which God prepared beforehand that we should walk in them. *Ephesians 2:10*

God does all this through His Word. In the Gospel He calls men. A Christian remembers his baptism and every day confesses that Jesus is his Lord. God strengthens his faith in the Holy Supper. With the Holy Spirit in him, a Christian strives to give himself totally to God and his fellowmen, as Paul urges:

> I appeal to you therefore, brethren, by the mercies of God, to present your bodies as a living sacrifice, holy and acceptable to God, which is your spiritual worship. *Romans 12:1*

God gives His people power to spend themselves for others. They do not struggle to be first. They do not overlook the needs and wants of their suffering neighbors. They are concerned about the spiritual growth of their fellow Christians. The result of faith in their lives is described by Paul:

> ✠ The fruit of the Spirit is love, joy, peace, patience, kindness, goodness, faithfulness, gentleness, self-control. *Galatians 5:22-23a*

What the holy God demands and what the merciful God promises form the pattern for the Christian life. In faith the Christian overcomes the world's evil with works of love.

CHRISTIAN VIRTUES ARE DIRECTED TO GOD AND TO OTHER PEOPLE

In response to God's love the Christian makes God Himself the object of the Christian's good deeds. To praise and thank Him, to support the teaching of His Word, and to be a witness for Him — these are good works directed to God.

Fellow human beings are the objects of a Christian's good deeds. He may show special concern for fellow Christians. However, he acts out his faith in God in love for all men. He asks, "How can I best bring Christ's love to them?" The Christian invests his time, energy, and money in this work.

GOD'S PEOPLE EVENTUALLY FIND A REWARD OF GRACE

Under the power of the Gospel the believer learns to love others unselfishly. He can lose his life serving his fellowman. He forgets about rewards for good deeds. But when he reaches heaven, he will discover that His Savior graciously remembers and rewards his good deeds. The Lord saves His people when they don't deserve it.

Prayer Thought—

I ask the Lord to grant me a growing faith
that I may in gratitude to Him live to His
glory and brighten my life with Christian
deeds of love.

May we Thy precepts, Lord, fulfill
And do on earth our Father's will
As angels do above;
Still walk in Christ, the living Way,
With all Thy children and obey
The law of Christian love.

Hymn 412, stanza 1

275

60

Growing as a Christian

Have you ever seen a dwarf lemon tree? It is very small and produces only a few lemons. People use it as a house plant for decoration. Japanese gardeners discovered that if they carefully cut back the roots and limbs of trees again and again, the trees stayed alive but stopped growing. Such trees are oddities.

There are dwarf people, too. Now and then a person is born whose glands do not work right. We are sorry for such people. There are some people, however, who make dwarfs of themselves. They grow to full size in body, but they neglect to grow in spirit. It is a tragedy when the new life which God begins in Christians at Baptism does not grow.

GOD EXPECTS HIS PEOPLE TO GROW SPIRITUALLY

Christians begin as "babes in faith." There is nothing wrong with that. The Lord Jesus showed special care for little children and for people who had newly come to faith. It is not God's plan, however, that His people remain babes in faith. He wants them to grow and become strong workers for Him.

God wants His people to grow in *knowledge*. A person may be a Christian and know only a few things about the Savior. But God has revealed many important things about Jesus and His saving work. He expects His people to get to know more and more. When the Christian church began, few people knew much, but Peter urged those early Christians:

✠ Grow in the grace and knowledge of our Lord and Savior Jesus Christ.
2 Peter 3:18a

St. Paul reminded his congregations that Christians were to grow in *understanding* God's plan and work for them. Like a teacher outlining a course of study, Paul said he expects that Christians—

May have power to comprehend with all the saints what is the breadth

276

and length and height and depth, and to know the love of Christ which surpasses knowledge, that you may be filled with all the fulness of God. *Ephesians 3:18-19*

Even wise and aged pastors must admit that they are still working on that assignment. No student ever graduates from the school of Christian knowledge.

God also expects His people to increase in *faith*. Faith can grow. The apostles said to the Lord at one time, "Increase our faith" (Luke 17:5). Paul rejoiced to see proofs of growing faith in his friends and told them:

> ✠ We are bound to give thanks always for you . . . because your faith is growing abundantly. *2 Thessalonians 1:3a*

God also expects His people to grow in *skills* that are useful in serving Him. The holy writer showed real disappointment over certain believers who failed to grow in the work of Christ's church.

> ✠ For though by this time you ought to be teachers, you need someone to teach you again the first principles of God's Word. *Hebrews 5:12*

THE WORD OF GOD NOURISHES AND CAUSES GROWTH IN A CHRISTIAN

God's people know that growth in understanding and faith is God's work in them. God has given His Word to create and nourish faith. His Word is more than facts and stories. It carries the life and power of God. Therefore Peter urged:

> ✠ Like newborn babes, long for the pure spiritual milk, that by it you may grow up to salvation. *1 Peter 2:2*

A baby drinks milk. As he grows, he begins to eat solid food. The Lord says He wants His people to get away from the baby bottle and begin to eat meat (Heb. 5:13-14). He reminds His people that they are not to be satisfied with a beginner's knowledge of the teachings of Scripture. He expects them to go on to study the more difficult doctrines. The apostle wrote that we are to go beyond the basic teachings such as are found in the Catechism:

> ✠ Therefore let us leave the elementary doctrines of Christ and go on to maturity, not laying again a foundation of repentance from dead works and of faith toward God, with instruction about ablutions, the laying on of hands, the resurrection of the dead, and eternal judgment. *Hebrews 6:1-2*

277

THE ENTIRE CHRISTIAN LIFE IS A TRAINING FOR SERVICE

The Christian life is on-the-job training. The Christian works for God and keeps on learning. As he learns he takes on more difficult tasks for God.

The growth of a Christian's faith and knowledge and skill is not just for himself. If it were, he might say: "I know enough to get to heaven. Why should I bother to learn more?" The answer is that we are not saved just to wait for heaven. Every Christian is enlisted in God's work corps. As older and more skillful Christians leave this world, there must be a constant supply of trained workers to fill the gaps in the ranks.

Because of the need for constantly growing Christians, God's people have found many ways to teach and train each other. They have written more books than anyone can count. They use modern teaching tools, such as projected pictures and tape recorders. They operate schools on many levels. Nursery classes, elementary schools, high schools, colleges, Sunday schools, Bible classes, and Bible institutes are examples of God's people at work learning to serve. The Christian knows that his calling in life is to serve in the army of the Lord.

Nourished by God's Word and aided by fellow Christians, God's people grow more like Christ until they—

> . . . all attain to the unity of the faith and of the knowledge of the Son of God, to mature manhood, to the measure of the stature of the fulness of Christ. *Ephesians 4:13*

Prayer Thought—

> I ask for wisdom to use every possible means to grow in knowledge and faith all through my life. I ask God to help me prepare for worthy tasks in His church.

> Ever be Thou our Guide,
> Our Shepherd and our Pride,
> Our Staff and Song;
> Jesus, Thou Christ of God,
> By Thine enduring Word
> Lead us where Thou hast trod,
> Make our faith strong.
> *Hymn 628, stanza 4*

279

61

The Christian Life of Worship

The scientist says there is no atmosphere on the moon. Yet space explorers expect to live there for long periods of time. How will they stay alive without air to breathe? It seems that problem has already been solved. Space travelers will take their own atmosphere with them. In their spacecraft and in special helmets they hope to be able to breathe air similar to that which we have on earth.

In a sense the Christian is out of place on this planet called earth. He is a citizen of heaven. His *body* is prepared to live in the atmosphere of

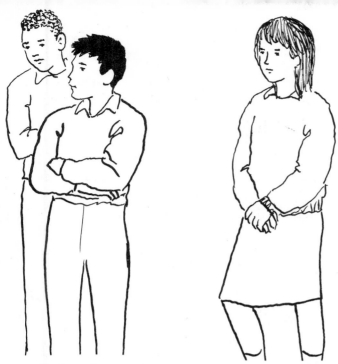

earth. His *spiritual* life, however, is in danger of being poisoned by the godless temptations around him. How does he protect himself? Very much like spacemen, he carries a bit of the atmosphere of his homeland with him at all times. To live always in the "atmosphere of heaven" may be called *worship*. Throughout the ages God's people have learned a number of ways to keep heaven's atmosphere with them.

THE CHRISTIAN CARRIES HEAVEN'S ATMOSPHERE IN HIS HEART

Each Christian lives his life in the presence of his God. He worships constantly. There are many times when he is not singing hymns or reading the Bible or praying. But he is aware of God's presence.

A child of God looks at life from God's point of view. At any time his constant worship may break forth into words of worship. As he enjoys the beauty of nature, he does not take it for granted. His heart and lips respond in thanks to God:

> ✠ O come, let us worship and bow down, let us kneel before the Lord, our Maker!
> *Psalm 95:6*

In temptation he does not ask, "Can I get away with it?" He recognizes that his life belongs to God. In every decision he tries to honor God by submitting to God's will. When he receives a special blessing, he doesn't

281

grab at it as if he deserved it. He sees it as a gift from God, and he is grateful. If the Christian receives praise, he admits that he is nothing without God. He gives God the credit, humbly saying:

> ⚕ Ascribe to the Lord the glory due His name; bring an offering, and come before Him! *1 Chronicles 16:29*

When the Christian looks at his home, his children, his health, or his money, he confesses that he is only a caretaker. God owns all these things.

With his heart attuned to God's will, the Christian recognizes God's greatness in all that he does. This is worship. His life itself is a hymn of praise to the Creator, Redeemer, and Sanctifier. The power that moves his life in God's ways is the power of the Holy Spirit.

THE CHRISTIAN KEEPS HEAVEN'S ATMOSPHERE IN HIS HOME

In his home the Christian worships with his loved ones. He strives to keep the poison of the world and Satan out of his home. He takes time for prayer and Bible reading. He adorns his home with pictures and symbols of the faith to mark it as a little outpost of heaven. He kneels to pray. He sings the songs of the heavenly homeland.

In the Christian home God is an honored Guest. His people speak to Him in prayer and listen when He speaks through His Word. When sin and weakness creep in, repentance and the power of God in faith drive it out. Each Christian family is the church, the body of Christ, within its own home. An important part of the family's business is the regular worship of God.

THE CHRISTIAN FINDS HEAVEN'S ATMOSPHERE IN WORSHIP WITH HIS FELLOW CHRISTIANS

Since the beginning of time, God's people have worshiped God in company with fellow believers. Joining their prayers and songs and hearing God speaking in His Word, they approach God in common faith. As they worship together, the redeemed people of God use whatever they can to shut out the world and prepare a heavenly atmosphere.

They prepare *holy places*. In times past they sometimes met under special trees. In days of persecution they met secretly at night in the burial caves of Rome. Whenever possible, God's people build houses of worship. With loving care they have built cathedrals and chapels in thousands of cities and villages.

In their houses of worship God's people place *holy things.* They use pulpits and altars. They use special colors to remind them of God's great acts for them. They have developed the pipe organ as an instrument with which to worship God. Workers in silver, gold, and other metals provide the vessels for use in celebrating the Sacrament. Pastors wear vestments of dignity. They can, of course, worship God without these holy things. Yet they use these things to show their adoration of God as Solomon did when he built the temple.

God's people also have their own *holy seasons.* They have arranged their own calendar to remind them of all that God has done for them. The Christian year is arranged around the four great holidays of Christmas, Easter, Pentecost, and Trinity. Each Sunday has its own name. A special part of the Gospel message is stressed on each Sunday.

To help them worship God, Christians have prepared *holy music.* The teachings of the Christian faith have been handed down in hymns and carols. Hymns are confessions and prayers set to music. Thrilling instrumental and choral music prepares their minds for worship.

The child of God in faith accepts the promises of forgiveness and life eternal. He claims citizenship in heaven for Jesus' sake. His life is a response to all that God has done for him. He worships in song and words of praise. He worships his God by the very way in which he lives.

Prayer Thought—

> I ask God to help me worship Him in word
> and deed and thought. I ask Him to grant
> me the joy of fellowship with Him in
> my worship at home and with my
> congregation.

> Praise to the Lord, the Almighty, the King of creation!
> O my soul, praise Him, for He is thy Health and Salvation!
> Join the full throng; Wake, harp and psalter and song;
> Sound forth in glad adoration!

Hymn 39, stanza 1

283

62

Living Witnesses of the Living Lord

Saul was going to get rid of the followers of Jesus. Even if he had to put them all in jail, he would stamp out this new faith. There was a nest of them in Damascus. On his way to round them up, Saul ran headlong into God's new plan for his life.

With a flash of light and a roll of thunder God reached down from heaven. "Saul, stop fighting Me," said Jesus. "I am choosing you to be on My side." Blinded and confused, Saul waited in Damascus. After 3 days Ananias came to explain what was happening.

> He said, "The God of our fathers appointed you to know His will, to see the Just One and to hear a voice from His mouth; for you will be a witness for Him to all men of what you have seen and heard."
> *Acts 22:14-15*

Saul became the apostle Paul. There was no doubt about why God had chosen him. Until the Roman executioner stilled his voice, Paul roamed the earth with one message. He spread the good news of God: "Believe in Jesus and be saved." Paul was a witness.

ALL CHRISTIANS ARE CHOSEN TO BE CHRIST'S WITNESSES

Like Paul, every Christian is chosen by God but the manner of choosing may not be as violent as it was with Paul. Yet by Baptism and His Word God reaches down to say, "I have chosen you." Why? God chooses people so that they may live with Him forever. Through His Son He takes away their sin. But He chooses them also to be His witnesses. This is true of every Christian.

It was true when God chose the nation of Israel. To His people God said:

> ✠ Fear not, for I have redeemed you; I have called you by name, you are Mine. . . . You are My witnesses. *Isaiah 43:1, 10*

The Lord chose the apostles and gave them special training to be His witnesses. Jesus plainly told them in the Upper Room:

> You also are witnesses. *John 15:27a*

The very last words Jesus spoke on this earth to all His followers were:

> ✠ You shall be My witnesses in Jerusalem and in all Judea and Samaria and to the end of the earth. *Acts 1:8b*

A witness is one who knows something and tells it. God has left a witness for Himself in His inspired Bible. But He also wants *living witnesses.* Therefore He puts His life into His people. The living Lord wants living spokesmen.

WE CANNOT BUT SPEAK

When Jesus ascended to heaven, 120 Christian believers saw Him go up into the clouds. Today about 700 million people call themselves Christian. God alone knows how many true believers there are today on earth and in heaven. Through the ages the witnesses have been at work.

Now the task belongs to us. We are the people chosen to witness for Christ in this age. By word and deed we are to be walking and talking witnesses. People can't see God. Many will not read the Bible. They can see us and hear us. Each Christian in his lifetime meets thousands of people. Will they hear from us the wonderful words of life? That is God's plan.

Alone, each Christian is only a single voice for God. Often that is all that is needed. Together, Christians can carry the message to the ends of the earth. That is what Jesus meant in His last words: ". . . to the end of the earth." The task is difficult. When a man can't do a job by himself, he works together with others. That's why Jesus told His people to work together. A Christian does not look upon his church as a place where *he* is served. It is a means by which he can multiply his voice of witness.

To carry out our task of witnessing is costly. It demands time, money, and effort. Let it cost! This is our reason for existing. In the face of the threats of those who would silence the voice of Christian witness, Jesus' followers say with the apostles:

✠ We cannot but speak of what we have seen and heard. *Acts 4:20*

WE ARE IN THE KING'S SERVICE

This world is a busy and tempting place. The young Christian is thoughtful as he looks ahead. "What will I be?" he asks. His earthly career will become known as time marches on. In this scientific world, some of the jobs which people will do 10 years from now have not yet been invented.

But one thing is sure: A Christian has been chosen by God. He is no longer an earthbound creature. He is marked for eternity. He has been bought by the blood of the Lamb of God. He is in touch with the Creator of the universe. He has a calling as an ambassador of the King of kings.

Forgiven by grace and guided by his Lord's Word, he moves down the years. Behind him follow those who have come to faith through his witness.

Someday he will see his last sunset in this world. On that day his Savior will take the veil from his eyes. Behold! It will not be a sunset at all—rather the sunrise of eternity! The trumpets of God and the chorus of the angels will sound the welcome of the homeland. With His cross-scarred hands the Lord will embrace His child and say, "I told you that you were Mine."

Prayer—

> Send, we beseech Thee, Almighty God,
> Thy Holy Spirit into our hearts that He
> may rule and direct us according to Thy
> will, comfort us in all our temptations and
> afflictions, defend us from all error, and
> lead us into all truth; that we, being
> steadfast in the faith, may increase in
> love and in all good works and in the end
> obtain everlasting life; through Jesus
> Christ, Thy Son, our Lord. Amen.

> God of grace and love and blessing,
> Thine alone shall be the praise;
> Give us hearts to trust Thee truly,
> Hands to serve Thee all our days.
> Lord, bestow Thy future blessing
> Till we join the heavenly host,
> There to praise and serve Thee ever,
> Father, Son, and Holy Ghost. Amen.
>
> *Hymn 640, stanza 4*

GIVE GOD THE GLORY